THE OXFORD INTRODUCTION
TO BRITISH HISTORY

General Editor: H. S. DEIGHTON

A
PORTRAIT OF BRITAIN
IN THE
MIDDLE AGES
1066–1485

BY

MARY R. PRICE

ILLUSTRATED BY

R. S. SHERRIFFS

OXFORD

Oxford University Press, Walton Street, Oxford OX2 6DP

LONDON GLASGOW NEW YORK TORONTO
DELHI BOMBAY CALCUTTA MADRAS KARACHI
NAIROBI DAR ES SALAAM CAPE TOWN SALISBURY
KUALA LUMPUR SINGAPORE HONG KONG TOKYO
MELBOURNE AUCKLAND

and associate companies in
BEIRUT BERLIN IBADAN MEXICO CITY

ISBN 0 19 832919 9

First published 1951
Reprinted from sheets of the first edition
1964, 1966, 1968, 1970, 1974, 1977, 1979, 1982

Printed in Hong Kong

GENERAL EDITOR'S PREFACE

THE inspiration of this series has been Mr. G. M. Young's *Victorian England: The Portrait of an Age*. A number of teachers suggested that Mr. Young's technique might usefully be adapted and used in a set of books designed as a History course for pupils from 11 to 15 or 16 in Grammar Schools. We have therefore attempted a double task. The books are intended for use as class text-books, and we have accepted the responsibility for providing enough information to meet the needs of classes preparing for the General Certificate of Education at Ordinary level. But it has been our purpose to give the children, along with this knowledge of the sequence of events, an understanding of the character of the periods—periods which may later be studied in greater detail in, for example, *The Oxford History of England*. We have thought of historical study as productive, not merely of knowledge, but of understanding. Thus we have regarded the period of four years for which the course is designed as providing, not only a minimum of historical information, but the beginning of the pupil's historical reading—and his introduction to the practice of applying historical knowledge to the understanding of life.

H. S. D.

PEMBROKE COLLEGE, OXFORD

AUTHOR'S PREFACE

THE material chosen for this book and the pattern of its presentation have stimulated both curiosity and individual research in children I have taught and I hope they will do the same for those who read it. I do not expect that they will satisfy every teacher. No book can or should ever do that. I have deliberately tried to resist the temptation which particularly besets those who teach history to include everything that I feel must be taught, since no book ought to attempt to take the place of the teacher.

Mr. Sherriffs's illustrations will repay close attention. They are not simply impressions. They are backed by his own knowledge of historical sources and by the advice of Mr. James Laver of the Victoria and Albert Museum and they, therefore, contain much useful teaching material.

M. R. P.

MILHAM FORD SCHOOL, OXFORD

CONTENTS

CONTENTS

1. Introduction

IN 1066 William, Duke of Normandy, launched his great (for those days) invasion force against England and made a successful landing. He was the last invader ever to force his way here and conquer the land with the points of sword and spear, although there were to be many more who were prepared to try, not only in the Middle Ages, but in the later days of bayonets and even of tommy-guns. Only three months later he was crowned William I, King of England, at Westminster, but it took six long years of fighting and working before he could really call himself master of the land and people. During those first difficult years, and indeed all through his whole reign (he died in 1087) William tried to find out as much as possible about his new subjects, how they lived, and worked, and managed their

HEADPIECE. Roman legionaries on the march in columns of four. They are carrying their 65 lb. of kit and are preceded by the standard-bearer. Their commander is on horseback and a centurion marches alongside. The kit included, beside weapons, several stockade posts, a mattock and spade, cooking pots, and rations

affairs. He was a very shrewd man, and he knew he must understand them if he was to remain firmly seated on his stolen throne and get a comfortable living from the land. Many were the questions he asked, either personally or through the royal officials he appointed and sent throughout the country to collect information.

A good deal of all that information was written down in the great book of the Domesday Survey which William caused to be made in 1085, and no doubt he was highly pleased with it. But nearly every one of us could have told him more than he ever knew about the England he had conquered. For it is now almost nine hundred years since he arrived and during that time many people interested in that far past before he came have delved and dug into it, and have discovered a great deal that William would probably have liked to know and never could.

First of all, the people of England in 1066 were already a very mixed lot. For over a thousand years different races with differing looks and languages had been arriving on these shores, usually coming first to raid and plunder and make off again quickly, but later to settle down and take possession. William and his Normans were the very last to come.

Before the days when Christ worked as a carpenter in the village of Nazareth, and the Roman legions controlled the Holy Land and all the other lands round the Mediterranean Sea, this country had been overrun by Celts. They were usually tall and fair, but they had intermarried with the earlier people of Britain and so some of their children were dark-haired and short. Thus the inhabitants of Britain were even then a mixed race. These Britons, as they were called, made a great impression on anyone who met them for the first time in battle, because on such important occasions they dyed their hair and moustaches red, and their arms and legs blue, with the juice of a small plant called woad. As a result their appearance was most startling, even terrifying, which was exactly what they wanted. But it is utterly wrong to think of them as red and blue savages dressed in hairy hearth-rugs. They were, in fact, rather well-dressed, clever, and artistic people, skilful in making beautiful jewelry, collars and bracelets and brooches of gold and silver, as well as handsome shields, and pottery of excellent shape and colour. Their clothes were made of many-coloured cloth, which probably looked very much like Irish or Scottish tartans, and we know this could only have been produced by fairly expert weavers. The men wore long loose trousers with short tunics and cloaks, and the women had longer tunics, almost to the ankles, and cloaks.

The Britons worshipped many gods, some of which they thought lived in trees and streams, and their priests, called Druids, were very powerful. They were a class set apart to lead the people. All knowledge, such as it was, was in their hands, and those who disobeyed their laws were burned to death. In their holy places, which were great circles of enormous stones like Avebury and Stonehenge, they held dramatic ceremonies, and before a tribe went to war they offered human sacrifices to please their gods. It was the Druids who taught that certain trees, like oak, ash, and thorn were magic, and that the mysterious-looking mistletoe was so sacred that it should only be cut at special times and with a golden knife.

The Britons lived chiefly by hunting, herding their flocks, and fishing, but they grew some wheat and oats for food, and also for making drink with which they loved to fuddle their brains. As they were related to the Celts, who lived in Gaul, they traded with them across the narrow seas which we call the

English Channel. Tin and gold, pearls, and slaves were the things they sold, and this merchandise was well known to the Romans when they conquered Gaul. The Romans also knew that the Celts from Britain were a perpetual nuisance, for they were always helping their conquered cousins to fight on and on against the legions instead of giving in, and at last Julius Caesar himself decided to go and find out what the misty island, which could be seen across thirty miles of salt water, was like. He hoped to subdue the troublesome Britons.

Caesar paid two visits, in 55 B.C. and again in 54 B.C., but they were not much more than raids and demonstrations of Roman power, and not very successful. However, nearly a hundred years later, the Emperor Claudius set out seriously on the business of conquering the island. It was not, at any rate to begin with, a very difficult task. For one thing, as you can see at once from the map, the east and south coasts, the coasts that face the mainland of Europe, are in most places low and easy to land on, with many sheltered havens, and rivers up which boats can sail. Only to the west and north is there a dangerous rock-bound coast. Besides, when once an invader had landed, there was at first nothing in his way worse than thick forests and marshes, and only when he came to the mountains of Wales and the north of England and Scotland did he meet any serious obstacles. For another thing, although the British were brave fighters, they were divided up into tribes or clans, and had no idea of presenting a united front to an enemy. Even the gallant efforts of leaders like Caractacus and Boudicca were no match in the end for the discipline and weapons of the Roman legions. And so, when in A.D. 43 the legions came the third time, the south and midlands were conquered without much difficulty. Wales and the north took much longer, and

AUGUSTINE'S MONKS
restoring the Roman church of St. Martin's at Canterbury
(see p. 17)

Scotland was never subdued. In fact the limit of the Roman power was marked by the great wall planned by the Emperor Hadrian and called after him, which marched across the wild and lonely moors of the north for seventy-three miles from sea to sea.

But farther south the Romans were supreme and in many places the British began to live their lives on the Roman pattern. Towns sprang up complete with baths, temples, and market-places, and country villas were built, the remains of which you can still explore at St. Albans and Bath, or at Chedworth in Gloucestershire. Many of the British took to speaking Latin, important men wore the great ceremonial cloak of the Romans, the toga, six yards long and two yards wide, and it became fashionable, if you were a rich man, to enjoy baths and to put central heating into your house. Life for most Britons was peaceful and orderly.

But as time went on Rome herself began to be in trouble and her power weakened. Barbarian peoples outside the empire took the opportunity to attack their old enemy, so that Rome, struggling now for her own life, paid less and less attention to the island on the very outskirts of her territory. And at the same time the part of Britain which is now England was much troubled itself by raiders from Scotland and by pirates from over the sea, and when in A.D. 410 word came from Rome that all the legions were to be withdrawn and no more would be sent, the Britons were left to defend themselves from these enemies, and were completely out of practice in doing so.

The next hundred and fifty years were a terrible time for them. From north-west Germany hordes of greedy raiders, Angles, Saxons, and Jutes, came upon the land in an almost continuous stream till no stretch of the low coast in the south and east was safe from them. At first probably these attackers were simply war-parties coming to raid and rob, and to destroy what they could not carry off, but soon they began to bring over their wives and families and to settle in groups and take possession. And everywhere they settled the bewildered Britons met their death or became sullen slaves to the invaders, or they fled to the west and north, to the difficult country in Cornwall and the mountains of Wales, the Lake District, and Scotland. Britain became the home of the third set of invaders, taking the name Engla-land from some of them—the Angles. First had come the Celts or Britons, as they came to be called, then the Romans, then the Anglo-Saxons, the English.

These English, terrible and ruthless as enemies—as of course they had to be—were kindly and good-natured in a rough way

ANGLO-SAXON ENGLAND

After A.D. 410, when the Romans were withdrawn, Britain lay exposed to the invaders from across the North Sea. Angles, Saxons, and Jutes came in increasing numbers till by the middle of the sixth century British resistance was broken, many Britons fled to the West, and their land was divided into seven Anglo-Saxon kingdoms: Northumbria, Mercia, East Anglia, Essex, Wessex, Sussex, and Kent (see p. 18)

among their own kin, as fond of eating and drinking as they were of fighting. They loved to gather round the house-fire in the evening and listen to stories and songs about the ancient heroes of their race, and about the great deeds they had done in battle. They were much more successful farmers than the Britons had ever been, for they cultivated and drained the more fertile lowlands of the country, cutting down the dense woods, and clearing the difficult jungle which covered the good soil. Many of them had come from foggy, barren lands, so no doubt they were entranced by their new home, a warm island with plenty of water, with soft delicate colours, and fertile little patches of cornland and pasture, and forests swarming with beast and bird of every kind.

Gradually almost every sign of the Romans disappeared. The towns stood empty and silent, for the English had no use for town life; and houses, temples, baths, and market-places fell into a state of ruin. First grass and then trees grew up and hid them, and the country villas too, so that when they have been rediscovered hundreds of years later they are many feet below ground and have to be dug out. It was as if a cloth had been passed over the face of Britain and all Roman marks wiped out, except the great roads, along which the legions had marched north, south, east, and west, and these remained, deserted for the most part, for the English used them little. The British refugees must, of course, have taken some knowledge of Latin and of Roman ways away with them into the west, but in those wilder parts they soon forgot.

One thing, however, they did treasure and keep alive, and that was the Christian faith. For just about a hundred years before the legions left Britain the Roman emperor Constantine granted freedom of worship to Christians, and soon afterwards the first churches were built in Britain, one, we know, at Canterbury and another at Silchester in Hampshire. They were few and tiny—the one at Silchester is a mere fourteen yards long and nine yards wide—and probably only a small number of Britons became Christians. But this small number carried their faith with them to their new homes, and it flourished. Yet they hated the English so much that they never passed on the good news of the Gospels to them, and the invaders went on worshipping the gods of their forefathers, Thor the thunderer, whose hammers could be heard banging in a terrifying way in the summer sky, Tiw the god of war, and the great Woden, chief of them all.

Britain was not the only country to suffer from fierce invaders during this time. All over Europe people were enduring similar or worse misery, and not merely for a few years either. This black period of history, when chaos took the place of Roman law and order, and kingdoms toppled, and cities were sacked, and thousands of people like you and me lived in misery, lasted for hundreds of years, from about A.D. 300 to 800. But through it all there was one body of men who managed to keep alive the ideas of mercy, peace, and quiet learning. That body was the Christian Church, and marvellous and divine indeed it must then have seemed to come across a priest or monk, a man who, if you were wounded, or poor, or terrified, would not brain you at one blow, or put you in fetters as his slave, but would give you bread and shelter and words of comfort in the name of God. It was this very Church that had been Rome's last and greatest gift to Britain. As time went on, Christian missionaries again and again went out to take their precious knowledge to pagan people, and two groups of them began at last to convert the English.

The first group came direct from Rome itself, led by St. Augustine and sent by Pope Gregory, the head of the Church. The second came by a much more roundabout way.

St. Augustine and his forty black-robed companions landed in Kent in A.D. 597, got leave from the king to rebuild the ruined little church at Canterbury, and began the long slow process of converting the English. Thirty-eight years afterwards the second and different set of missionaries began to trickle into the north. They came from a monastery on the island of Iona which had been built by an Irish monk called Columba. They were cheerful, lovable men, Aidan and Cuthbert and many more like them who tramped over the hills and moors to preach to the men of the north, living the hardest and simplest of lives. Gradually through the Roman and Irish missionaries the Christian faith spread throughout the land. Small churches were built and monasteries like Jarrow, Whitby, and Canterbury, and the English began to understand the importance of mercy, justice, and peace, and of books and music.

By the end of the eighth century there was comparative peace in England. Indeed, the English in this century were actually civilizing the people of Germany, and we may say that they were the most peaceful, as well as the most important, of all the peoples of western Europe. The descendants of the one-time raiders had settled down in the seven kingdoms called Northumbria, Mercia, East Anglia, Kent, Essex, Sussex, and Wessex, and few remembered that their forefathers had ever lived anywhere else. The remaining Britons stayed in Cornwall, Wales, and the Lake District, fighting among themselves but not interfering much with the rest of the country. But there were still two more waves of invaders to come before William and his Normans, and in A.D. 793 the first of these arrived.

VIKING FLOTILLA APPROACHING ENGLAND

The ships are being steered by an oar at the stern, and the shields are hung
along the gunwales

Long black ships with bright shields hung along their gunwales, and filled with fighting men appeared off the unprotected coasts in the east and south. They came from Denmark, Norway, and Sweden, and the tough, pagan warriors they carried were known as Northmen or Vikings. England was only one of the countries which these Northmen attacked. Some went by way of the Baltic Sea to Russia, and then south to Constantinople, others braved the Bay of Biscay and reached the Mediterranean, and the most daring of all sailed to Iceland and Greenland, and landed, five hundred years before Columbus, on the coast of North America.

England, Scotland, Ireland, and France bore the brunt of their attacks. Like the Angles, Saxons, and Jutes before them, they first came only as raiders but later, attracted by the green and fertile country, began to settle. The seven English kingdoms struggled and fought against them but soon lay as helpless as the Britons had five hundred years before. Not until the Northmen had been doing their worst for nearly a hundred years did anyone in England offer really stiff resistance. In the year 871 a young man called Alfred became the king of Wessex. Although he was only twenty-three, and all his life was delicate and ailing, he rallied the despairing English under his standard of the golden dragon, and beat the Northmen out of his own kingdom and eastward across the Roman road called Watling Street, which runs from London to Chester. Not content with this Alfred determined to protect Wessex from further attacks. He built a fleet—the first English king to do so—of ships longer and swifter than the Northmen's, he built burghs, or fortified towns, at intervals along his boundaries. And he also began a new method of calling up men for his army. It was not enough he thought, faced with the danger of the Northmen, to rely solely on his royal men-at-arms and personal followers. All Englishmen should be ready to help if necessary. So he ordered that every man, save only cripples, young boys, and the very old, must have a spear, a helmet, and a shield, and be prepared to fight. This army was called the *fyrd*, and was rather like the territorial army is today except that everyone had to belong to it.

Alfred died in A.D. 899. He was not only a soldier but a civilizer too. He founded schools, rebuilt ruined monasteries, and caused the laws and customs of his land to be collected and written down. For nearly eighty years his sons and grandsons went on fighting the Northmen and gradually subdued them, so that the kings of Wessex became the kings of all England and the Northmen settled down among the English. But there was still one more wave of invaders to come and, in 978, when the feeble Ethelred the Redeless was on the throne, it came. Once more the black ships appeared, and year after year the North-men marched insolently through the country, killing, burning,

ALFRED THE SAILOR

King Alfred was one of the first to realize the importance of a navy for the defence of England

and robbing. No Alfred came to the rescue this time, and Ethelred's only idea of ridding the land of the enemy was to pay them large sums of gold to go away. They went—for a time—but naturally returned for more and more money, or dane-geld, as it was called. In the late winter of 1013 Ethelred in despair fled to Normandy to his wife's family. He returned in 1014 and made a last attempt to drive the Northmen out of his kingdom, without success, and two years later he died. Canute the Dane became King of England. Canute was no mere pirate but a wise and strong man who ruled England for nineteen years, and when he died in 1035 he seemed to have settled his family safely on the throne, for he had two sons to follow him. Yet within eight years both of them were dead and in 1042 Edward, son of Ethelred, returned to the land of his fathers and became king.

Edward was the last of the old royal house of Wessex to be king of England and a more unsuitable man for the position could hardly be imagined. This shy, short-sighted man, with hair so fair that it looked like silver, had always longed to become a monk and to live in quiet and peace, giving all his energy to prayer and reading. Yet his fate was to rule England at a very difficult time when a firm and ruthless king was needed to unite and strengthen her and keep her safe from enemies. As it was, he wavered perpetually between two parties, his own friends from Normandy where he had been brought up, and the English party led by the great Earl Godwin and his family. The struggle for power over the melancholy Edward went back and forth between Norman courtiers and English thanes, but for the last thirteen years of Edward's reign the English were the more powerful and the man on whom the king relied most was Harold, son of Godwin. So great was his influence, both with Edward and with Englishmen generally, that many believed he would inherit the crown, for the king had no children. As the year 1065 waned Edward lay dying in his palace. The only thing he seemed to care about was the finishing of the stately new church of Westminster which was the last dream of his life. But people round him were much more interested in who he would declare his heir, and anxiously they waited. It is said that just before he died he murmured the name of Harold. Then many Englishmen rejoiced to think that one of themselves was to wear the crown, but others were angry. Great earls, who were jealous of Harold and his family, were bitterly hostile. Among them were Edwin and Morcar, men who held huge estates in the north of England, and who would be dangerous foes indeed if they should decide to oppose the new king.

But Harold had another and more deadly foe, William, duke

WESTMINSTER ABBEY, 1066
Recreated from the Bayeux Tapestry

of Normandy. He was second cousin to King Edward, and because the Confessor had a great love for Normandy, he had been a welcome visitor to the English court, and probably he had been told by Edward, who had no children, that he should succeed him as king. And this William was passionately anxious to do. He was descended from the roving Vikings, and the very spirit of those sea-wolves lived on in him. All his life he had known danger, and as a young boy had fought hard to keep his dukedom. So well had he succeeded that he was not only complete master of his Norman subjects but also one of the greatest men alive at the time. He was fearless, hard, and ruthless, and he was determined to be king of England as well as duke of Normandy.

When he heard that Harold had been named king, William

was almost mad with rage and jealousy, and all the more so because he had expected Harold to be one of his own best helpers. For not long before the Confessor's death William had made a bargain with Harold over this very matter. Harold had been shipwrecked on the coast of Normandy and had been taken to William's court. Being a very important person in England he was something of a prize and for a time William would not let him go home. At last, however, he was set free after having sworn an oath to help William to obtain the English crown. At least that is what William afterwards declared, and he said, moreover, that Harold had sworn on the bones of a holy saint which made his oath specially binding. No one knows exactly what happened between the two men, but it was enough for William to declare Harold a traitor and oath-breaker, and to begin preparations for the invasion of England as soon as he heard that Harold himself was to succeed Edward the Confessor.

2. William of Normandy comes to England

ON 29 September 1066 at nine o'clock in the morning William, duke of Normandy, landed on the coast of Sussex not far from the towering white cliff of Beachy Head. His ship, the *Mora*, which had been given to him by his wife, was probably the very first of the long low Norman craft to touch the shore, for at dawn that morning he had been so well ahead of the rest of his fleet that he had ordered the anchor to be cast in mid-Channel, and, while waiting for the other ships to come up, had calmly eaten his breakfast 'as it had been in his own hall'. As the keel of the *Mora* grounded William leapt ashore, the first of all the Norman host, and as he landed he stumbled, and fell upon the shingle so hard that his nose began to bleed and his hands were covered with sand. For a moment, perhaps, his sudden fall sent a shock through the ranks of his followers and they asked themselves if this accident was an evil omen foretelling failure and

HEADPIECE. Normans building transport. From the Bayeux Tapestry

25

Right. The double invasion. Harald Hard-rada from Norway, William the Conqueror from Normandy.

Below. William's route from Hastings to London. It was important to make a detour as the Thames at London was very marshy and there was only one bridge, which could be easily defended

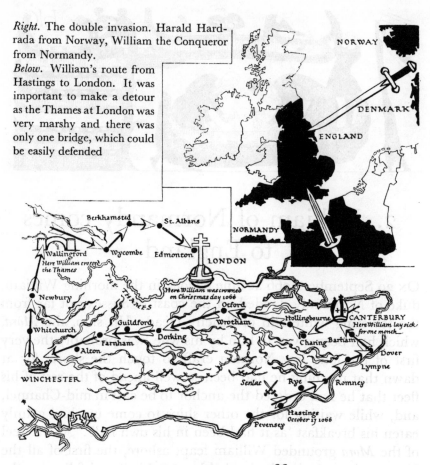

THE INVASIONS OF 1066

loss. But William quickly rose and laughed, and cried, 'By the splendour of God I have taken seisin of England'. For in those days when a man obtained some new land he was often given a small portion of its soil as seisin—a mark of possession—and William had already some of England's soil on his hands. Then, with shouts and cheers, the Norman army began to disembark and unload their ships. They were close to the old stronghold of Pevensey whose walls had been built by the Romans, and you can still stand on these walls to-day and look out on the strip of coast where they landed, though the sea has retreated since 1066 and some flat marshy fields lie between you and the water's edge. Within the walls of Pevensey William ordered a wooden fort to be built as soon as the ships were unloaded.

This was a great moment for the Normans, coming, as it did, after months of preparations. All through the summer these preparations had gone on across the hundred-mile stretch of sea which separates the coast of England from Normandy, and fortunately we know a good deal about them. For, if you go to the Norman town of Bayeux, you can see in the museum, just opposite the cathedral, the famous Bayeux tapestry. It is a strip of canvas, many yards long and about eighteen inches wide, embroidered with wonderfully clear pictures of the whole business. It was made to hang round the walls of the cathedral, and it is said that William's wife, Matilda, and her ladies sat and stitched it while the conquest was going on. Anyhow, whoever did it must have known a great deal about the whole conquest, and must have watched the workmen and soldiers labouring away in the little towns round the mouth of the River Dives, where the invasion fleet was gathered, because the tapestry shows so exactly the kind of things that went on.

First of all, William had to build enough ships, perhaps

'700 ships save 4' as a writer of the time says, to carry his whole army across to England, as well as their horses and provisions, and that was no easy task. In the tapestry you see men felling trees for these ships, cutting them into planks and smoothing them, and others working on the boats themselves. You can recognize the tools they are using if you know a little about carpentry. There are also men carrying sacks of food and casks of wine, and armour of all kinds to be stowed away on board. The armour and weapons were very important. In battle the Normans wore a tunic and breeches, probably all in one piece, made of leather, or thick padded material with small rings of iron or overlapping scales of metal sewn all over. This garment had a hood, which they pulled up over the head for protection, and over that was worn an iron helmet, closely fitting and with a strong nose guard, called a 'nasal'. Their shields were shaped like kites, and the long pointed ends protected a man's thighs as he rode among his enemies, for many Normans went into battle on horseback. They fought with long spears, swords, and bows and arrows, and it is clear from the Bayeux tapestry that plenty of armour and stacks of weapons were carried in the ships, as well as wine and food. Horses too were packed on board.

All this equipment was very different from that of the English. If they wore armour at all it was like the Normans', but far fewer of them did, for, while most of William's army were trained soldiers, most of Harold's were not. They usually carried round shields and short swords, and they fought on foot with the huge battle-axes of their forefathers which, with luck, could cut off a horse's head at one blow. But a mounted man—and many of the Normans were mounted—had an advantage over a foot-soldier wielding such a weapon, for he could get in a deadly

THE LAST STAND OF HAROLD'S BODYGUARD
on the hill where now stands the Abbey of Battle (see pp. 35-6)

thrust with his long spear as the axe was being swung up for the blow. Then, too, the English seem to have had no archers in their army, which is odd considering that later on they were to be so famous for their bowmen. It is important to remember this because the arrows of the Normans did great damage among the English at the Battle of Hastings. Not all Harold's men were armed properly, many fought only with pitchforks, axes, or even the stout poles of oak or ash that they might use in their everyday life.

These preparations of men, arms, and food, were not the only ones that William had made before setting sail. He had also been collecting good wishes and blessings. The most important of these came from the Pope, the head of the Christian Church. He and William were both anxious to see the Church improved everywhere in Europe, so that its buildings were well cared for, its services reverently performed and, above all, that the priests and monks of all ranks should set an example of goodness, learning, and hard work. In Normandy William had been busy building new churches and monasteries—the Normans were great builders—and encouraging the clergy to live decent lives, and he was determined to do the same in England if he conquered it, for there the churches were often badly neglected, and many priests were unable to read and write and far keener on hunting than on preaching the Gospel of God. Then, too, Harold had sworn upon the bones of certain holy saints that he would support William in his claim to the English throne and he had clearly broken his oath. It is true that he may have been tricked into swearing it, and no one can be sure exactly what the promise was, but an oath was a most sacred and binding thing, and the Pope was bound to declare against Harold the oath-breaker. So, when the duke asked for a blessing on his expedition, promising at the same time to reform the English Church, the Pope gave it, and also sent William a holy ring to wear, and a special banner which was hung in the duke's own ship the *Mora* in a most conspicuous position.

William felt satisfied that no one of importance would challenge the goodness of his cause, or dare to help the faithless Harold, and his army felt they were fighting in a war which God would certainly bless. So, on the Norman side of the Channel, excitement grew and men's hearts were high, both at the prospect of battle and of the rewards of good English land which they expected. All through that summer, too, a strange star with a long gleaming tail of light appeared in the night sky. It was a comet, which we now know as Halley's comet, but it seemed weird and terrible to people in those days. They felt that it surely foretold that great things were about to happen. The Normans were quite certain that it prophesied a victory for them, and so even when their sailing was delayed by bad weather, much as the Anglo-American invasion of France was held up in the summer of 1944, they remained quite keen and confident.

On the other side of the Channel the star was also seen by Englishmen as they watched and waited, but to them the sight brought fear and anxiety. For in many ways they were not so well prepared as the Normans for the coming struggle. To begin with, although the Witan had chosen Harold as king and he had already been crowned, there were, as we saw, some great thanes who were jealous and disloyal. Among these were the earls of the north, Edwin and Morcar, and Harold's own brother Tostig. These men were not at all sure that it would pay them to help Harold in an invasion. It might be more profitable to help the invader. Then, too, William was not the only foreigner planning to seize the throne. The king of Norway, Harald (spelt with an *a*), had also prepared a fleet and an army. In fact he arrived before William did, and landed in Yorkshire on the banks of the River Ouse on 20 September, and Harold's jealous brother Tostig was with him. This meant that Harold (with an *o*) and some of his army were suddenly called away from their watch on the south coast to fight the invader in the north. On 25 September he reached York, and after trying to win Tostig over to his side he fought the men of Norway at Stamford Bridge and was victorious. The king of Norway and Earl Tostig were both killed and the invaders driven in flight to their ships. They had come with three hundred of these, but so many men were killed that only twenty-four ships sailed back to Norway.

Now this was a great victory for Harold of England, but it was a costly one. To begin with the best of his trained men or housecarls had been killed, and the remainder were very tired and in sore need of sleep and rest. And, as ill luck would have it, while all this was happening, the weather in the English Channel, which had been holding up the Normans, cleared. They set sail at once, and news reached Harold that William had landed on the unguarded coast of Sussex. Marching as hard as men and horses could go, the English turned south and made for London to meet a more terrible invader than the king of Norway.

Harold himself and the fittest of his bodyguard reached London in four days, but the rest of the army trailed more slowly after him, and it is very likely that some of them never saw him again. After waiting for a week collecting any fighting men he could, he again set out, this time to meet William. He had only his housecarls and some of the *fyrd*, or army, of the south-eastern counties, and it was a dangerously small force. Edwin and Morcar never appeared at all. They preferred to wait and see which of the two sides proved the stronger, and therefore the more profitable to join after the conflict. They had no thought at all of fighting to save England from an invader. Others, too, besides Edwin and Morcar, did not join Harold's army, among them the men of the south-west, Wiltshire, Dorset, Devon, and Somerset. This was chiefly because it was always difficult to collect men to fight just at the end of the harvest, a vital time when everyone was busy getting in the precious corn which would stand between them and hunger in the coming winter. There was no regular paid army in those days. Thanes and housecarls were trained to fight, but the rest were just farmers, and very reluctant to leave their homes and go off to some strange part of England to fight and perhaps to die. Every-

NORMAN BARON AND ENGLISH THEGN
Hundreds of English landowners were turned out by Normans to whom
William I gave their manors

one thought much more about their own particular small part
of England than about the country as a whole. They felt they
were men of Kent, or of Wessex, or of Northumbria rather than
Englishmen, and they had no patriotic feeling for the whole
country. Now, of course, if William had appeared on the coast
of Dorset, say at Weymouth, then the men of south-west
England would have left their harvest-fields in a hurry and tried
to resist him, but as it was, only the people of the south-east
realized the terrible danger that had come upon England by
sea, others did not understand the emergency. There was
nothing like the united spirit which five hundred years later set
the bonfires flaming from end to end of the land, warning men
of the approach of the Armada in July 1588.

It would have been difficult even for a wise and patient leader to decide what to do, whether to fight William at once, hoping for a victory which would attract waverers as well as drive out the Normans, or whether to hold back, waiting for reinforcements to gather slowly, content to harry William's rear and cut off his retreat to his ships and Normandy. Harold was not particularly wise or patient, but he was brave and swift, and he preferred a speedy meeting with the enemy. And so he chose a hill-top seven miles from Hastings, bare save for 'a hoar (old) apple tree', and drew up his men in close ranks to wait for the attack. It was a good position, for the Normans were at the disadvantage of having to ride or scramble up the hill to fight. The English were massed together with their best-armed men in front to bear the brunt of the attacks, and so closely did they stand that they presented a wall of shields which was impossible to break through. In these ranks fought Harold and two of his brothers, Gyrth and Leofwine, and over their heads floated the standard of Wessex embroidered with a great gold dragon, and Harold's own banner which bore a picture of a fighting man. The battle began early in the morning on a Saturday and raged all through the day, and Bayeux tapestry is again most useful in showing the details of the struggle. Usually the English are shown with battle-axes, or else without armour, and Harold himself is easily recognized by his long drooping moustache— the Normans were clean shaven. Spears flew through the air and arrows fell in showers like stinging hail, and men hacked and hewed with swords, and horses crashed down the steep sides of the hill. Once at least the Normans turned tail and would have fled from that terrible shield-wall on the top, but only William's determination and fury rallied them. But in the end two things wore down the English strength. The ceaseless arrows of the Normans fell everywhere amongst them and they had nothing to compare with them save stones hurled by hand. And twice at least the Normans pretended to fly and, in spite of all Harold's shouts and orders, Englishmen broke out of their ranks and pursued them, only to be turned upon and killed before they could get back to their places. Gradually the shield-wall thinned, the great axes rose and fell more weakly, the Normans pressed on and at last Harold was killed by an arrow, his body-guard lay dead around him, and the remnants of his army fled from the hill-top and wearily trailed away into the darkness to hide in the woods or to try to reach their homes. The two standards were pulled down by the Normans, and William set up the blessed banner of the Pope, and gave thanks to God for his first and greatest victory on English soil. Then he left the battlefield and returned to Hastings.

William's Standard overshadowing the
Dragon of Wessex (Bayeux)

3. William takes firm hold of England

THE day after the Battle of Hastings Duke William gave orders for the Norman dead to be buried, and he sent off Harold's torn and tragic banner of the fighting man as a present to the Pope. No one quite knows what happened to Harold's body, one story says that it was buried in secret under the sand and rocks of the sea-shore by order of the duke, who, mocking at his dead foe, said he might lie and guard the shore of England which he had failed to do when he was alive. But another story says that William allowed Harold's mother to take away the corpse to Waltham Abbey, where the monks gave it an honourable burial, and carved upon the tombstone the words *Harold Infelix*, Harold the Unhappy. Later on William built a monastery on the site of his victory and called it Battle Abbey, and the high altar of the abbey was placed on the very spot where

HEADPIECE. Norman castle on motte

Harold fell. If you visit the scene of the battle of Hastings now you can see some of the monastic buildings still standing, but the church itself is in ruins. Also the hill where the shield-wall held out so strongly is no longer bare but covered with trees and not much like it was in 1066.

William stayed at Hastings for a short time, in the wooden castle which his men had built, and which you can see in the Bayeux tapestry. It must have been made of some of the wood brought over from Normandy, and was set upon a high mound of earth. The men in the tapestry are very busy working at the mound, throwing soil and stone on to it and patting down its sides. Two of them, however, have got behind their foreman's back and are having a private battle of their own and trying to settle the matter with their spades! The Normans naturally expected to hear quite soon of another English army drawn up to meet them and bar their way to London, but nothing happened. No other leader appeared in place of Harold, and the people of Sussex and Kent lay low, stunned and sorrowful. At last William set off from Hastings and began to march towards London. First he went to Romney, then Dover, then Canterbury, each town giving in with little or no resistance. At Canterbury the duke fell ill and was delayed for a month, which was a golden opportunity for Englishmen to rally their forces against him. But still nothing happened, and as soon as he was fit the duke continued his journey, taking a roundabout way, and leaving a terrible trail of burned and wasted country behind him. At Berkhamstead he was met by an embassy of peace, sent by all the most important people who were left in London, and offering him the crown of England, as heir to Edward the Confessor. Then the Conqueror entered the city, and on Christmas Day 1066 he was crowned in the great church of

Westminster which had been built by the Confessor. The coronation service was far from peaceful, for in the middle a great tumult arose outside the church, and most of the congregation, fearing an ambush, left their places and rushed out to see what was happening. There they found a confused and violent scene, for a number of the duke's soldiers, believing that mischief was afoot, had set fire to some wooden houses, and an armed brawl had begun between Normans and English. It was nothing very serious, but it might easily have been a great attack for all William knew, as he heard the shouts and the crackling of fire, and saw the glint of flames through the door of the minster. But, nothing daunted, that 'stark man' remained calmly at the altar while the archbishop of York hastily placed the crown upon his head and finished the service. William's courage was not easily shaken.

So far, so good, for him, but it was hardly to be expected that one battle and one raiding march would really be enough to subdue the English and conquer their land. More resistance was bound to come. At first the people waited, watching uneasily, yet hopefully, to see how William acted. After all, thought many Englishmen, Edward the Confessor had been half a Norman, and they were used to hearing and seeing Frenchmen in the land, and often in the very highest positions about the king, without it troubling them very much. Perhaps William's rule might be the same—a French-speaking king with favourites from Normandy around him, but with Englishmen undisturbed holding as before their old lands, rank, and positions. But all who hoped thus, and indeed most Englishmen did so, soon began to find out that things were not to be at all the same under William. He at once began to turn out English landowners, great and small, and English clergy from their houses, and

THE REBELLION AT ELY

Hereward's men were expert at finding their way among the waterways and marshes
surrounding Ely, and they harried the Normans greatly (see p. 42)

estates, and churches, and to put his Normans in their places.
In this way he rewarded his followers as he had promised, and
also he weakened his foes, for in those days a man's wealth
depended on the size of his estates, and a great landowning
noble could be as powerful as the king himself. Soon it became
perfectly clear to everyone that 'the Normans are the high men
of England, and the low men the English'. Here and there, as
at Hastings, men were forced to labour at making great earthen
mounds and building castles, first of wood, but later of stone,
upon their summits, from which there rode forth armed Normans to watch and dominate the land. In London, where the
Tower was built, and up and down the country, at Norwich,
Bristol, Hereford, Lincoln, York, Cambridge, and many other
places, the English cursed as they toiled at the strongholds of

their new masters. The process, beginning in the south, went on steadily and ruthlessly—turn out the English, put in the Normans, and fortify the important places. In 1085 William had a great record of all England made, called the Domesday Book, and from it you can see how thoroughly the system worked, for you can read the names of the new Norman lords of villages and towns, and of the English men who were turned out. Here is an example, 'Aluric, sheriff of Huntingdon had a house in the time of King Edward [the Confessor] which William the King took and afterwards gave to his wife and sons'.

Sometimes, if the people resented the arrival of the foreigners, their houses were torn down and burned, and they fled homeless and starving into the woods and marshes; sometimes, if the new lord simply wanted more land, their houses were destroyed. At Lincoln, for instance, one hundred and sixty-six dwellings disappeared just 'on account of the castle' which was built there. This was the sort of thing that drove the English to resist, and so it was that William was troubled for years with armed revolts throughout the land, and his control grew only slowly. Three of the rebellions were particularly serious. One was at Exeter in 1067 where Harold's mother and her remaining sons had their headquarters, and where the citizens endured a siege of eighteen days before they gave in. William showed the people of Exeter more mercy than he ever did to rebels afterwards, perhaps he did not at first want to make more enemies than absolutely necessary!

The next was in the north which proved much tougher than Exeter. Three times did William march to York to subdue that city, and the third time he found not only the people of the north, but also a large army from Denmark which had come to help. It was a moment of great danger for him, for the landing

THE MAKING OF DOMESDAY BOOK, 1086

William I sent commissioners about the country to ask questions about every
existing manor. (Figures reconstructed from the Bayeux Tapestry)

of the Danes had put heart into many Englishmen, and in Devon, Dorset, Cornwall, and other places, the fires of rebellion flared up. But William proceeded to defeat the northern forces, retake York, and then to wreak terrible revenge on the people. For two months he harried the countryside, burning, killing, and destroying, till hundreds of villages lay utterly desolate, and refugees fled to the high moors and hills where they starved to death or perished from the bitter cold winter. Again and again in Domesday Book beside the descriptions of Yorkshire villages are written the words 'It is waste', and it is no wonder that the north lay quiet after such punishment, and 'men bowed their heads for meat in the evil days'.

The last important rebellion was in 1070 in the fen-land, at Ely. There, on a strip of dry land about eight miles long, surrounded by water and treacherous marshes through which only the local people could find a safe way, the English, led by Hereward the Wake, lord of the manor of Bourne, prepared to defy William. It was an excellent place to make a stand, being in those days really the 'Isle of Ely'. Water was no problem to Hereward and his men, nor was food, for the island was well supplied. A writer of the time tells us that, 'It is remarkable for its beasts of the chase, and very rich in flocks and herds. In the eddies at the watergates innumerable eels are caught, also pike, pickerels, perch, roach, burbots and lampreys. Many people say that salmon are also caught there, and the royal fish, the sturgeon. There one can find geese, teal, coots, didappers, watercrows, herons, and ducks more than a man can number in winter or at moulting time.' There was certainly plenty for the English to eat when William brought up his soldiers to lay siege to the place, and Hereward was a brave man and a good leader. But in spite of this well-chosen stronghold and the courage of the men who defended it, the rebellion came too late. The garrison of Ely had to beat William in battle if they were to do any good, it was not enough merely to hold out against him. Besides, the rest of England now lay quiet, no help could be expected from other rebellions breaking out behind William's back, and he could give his whole attention to the siege. He tried first to reach the stronghold by building a wooden causeway through the water. But Hereward's men stole out at night and burned it. He set up a wooden tower with a witch on the top to shout curses on the men of Ely in the hope of frightening them into yielding. But Hereward's night watchers burned the tower and the witch too. At last, however, the stubborn persistence of William, and probably the uncomfortable memory of the harrying of the north, began to make the English waver. What might be their terrible fate if they held out longer? Then, secretly, someone crept out from Ely and showed William and his men the way to reach the island, the Normans overwhelmed the garrison, Hereward fled, and the rebellion was over.

So gradually William made good his hold on England, largely because the English were divided among themselves, and their great men, jealous of each other, made no united front against him. Bit by bit the Conqueror settled his Frenchmen everywhere, and began to organize the country as he wished. First he claimed that every inch of the land belonged to the crown and from it he then granted estates to his most important supporters. Some of these men were earls, some barons, and some were bishops or abbots. But no matter how great they were, they all had to do homage to the king for the land,[1] that is, they knelt humbly before him, put their hands between his, and said: 'I become your man from this day forward, of life and limb and

---

[1] See the illustration on page 49.

earthly worship, and unto you I shall be true and faithful and shall hold faith for the lands I hold of you.' They also had to be ready to come to the king's court if he wanted to take counsel with them, and ask their advice, and this meeting was called the Great Council. These great tenants did not only pay money rents for their estates, they promised to give service to the king, and usually it was military service. Each had to supply a number of fully armed knights in time of war, and, unless he was a bishop or abbot, to fight himself too, and in this way the king could collect an army when he needed it. His tenants also gave him a certain amount of money, and what were called dues, such things as hounds and sparrowhawks for hunting, weapons of all sorts, and even herrings, and scarlet hose! Great landowners did not keep all their estates, which were often enormous, for themselves, but let out part to other lesser men in return for the same sort of service and dues as they owed the king. This curious method of holding land in return for service is called feudalism, and it was used in England all through the Middle Ages. There was so little money to pay rents with, that men had to give service in exchange for their land.

This sytem could be dangerous sometimes. For instance, if a great tenant was able to raise a hundred fighting men from his land to fight for the king, he might also be tempted to use them against the king at times. But William was shrewd enough to see this possibility, and though he granted vast estates to some men they were usually scattered, a village here, and another some way off, so that the mere collecting of his own tenants by a treacherous baron would be a lengthy business, and news of it probably would come to the king's ear in time for him to strike first. Nor could a baron easily escape paying his other dues to the king, for William knew too much about England

WILLIAM I HUNTING

The figures and the tree are reconstructed from the Bayeux Tapestry

for men to cheat him. Most of the knowledge came from the Domesday Survey which the Conquerer, after 'very deep speech with his wise men about this land', caused to be made in 1085–6. He sent men into every shire to gather information about the size of villages, how many people lived there, who held land, what they should give the king each year, and even how many pigs, cows, and sheep each man had. When all these details had been collected, 'the writings were brought to him', and from them William certainly knew a great deal about the land and what it was worth, and even where every fishpond lay and where the hawks nested in the country he had conquered.

William also remembered his promise to reform the Church, and he lost no time in beginning this. He turned out the English archbishop of Canterbury, an unworthy, treacherous fellow called Stigand, and put his own friend and counsellor, Lanfranc, there. Lanfranc made an excellent archbishop, and though he thought very little of Englishmen, he treated them fairly and won their respect. Many other high positions went to Norman priests and monks, and some of these were not so scrupulous as Lanfranc, and indeed often no better than the men whose places they took. The monks of the famous abbey at Glastonbury in Somerset refused to obey their new abbot, Thurstan, when he tried to make them sing new-fangled French chants, and he hounded them round the monastery with knights and archers, and even chased them into the church where some were killed and others wounded. But this was unusual. Thurstan was sent back to his own monastery in Normandy in disgrace. Other bishops and abbots were more like soldiers than clergy, not only did they send armed knights to wage war for the king in return for the land they held, but they fought themselves with great keenness whenever a chance came. But whatever their faults they were not lazy, and many were devout men and good scholars, and they were as anxious as the king to strengthen the Church. The Normans were great builders, and so, besides the detested castles, new churches were raised all over England. Some were great cathedrals and abbeys, like Winchester, York, and St. Albans, and others, like Kilpeck in Herefordshire, were sturdy little parish churches. All were in the style which the Normans brought from France, with round-headed arches and round pillars, and many of them have lasted till today. There were also changes in the monasteries, and English monks were expected to lead much stricter lives, to fast regularly, and to attend all the services which were spread through the day and night. They had to work harder at the tasks set them, and on no account leave the monastery without leave.

In order to keep the clergy up to high standards of behaviour, and also to make other people realize that they were set apart from ordinary men because of their special work of teaching about God, William set up Church law-courts where their misdeeds were judged and punished separately.

Of course these changes were unpopular, especially the presence of so many foreigners at court, in the Church, and in castles and in villages everywhere, men who despised anyone unable to speak French, and who thought the English a set of uncouth barbarians. Harsh and greedy they were, and greatly feared, and none more so than their lord and master, William, who ordered terrible punishments for all who angered or disobeyed him. The Conqueror's greatest joy was in hunting the hare, the fox, the wild boar, and especially the 'tall deer', and he had great forests kept for his royal sport. One of these, the New Forest in Hampshire, where he hunted whenever he was staying at Winchester, was made by taking over sixty villages and miles of farm land. Barns, churches, houses—everything— was destroyed, and the miserable people turned out. For some the only way to keep alive was to catch some of the king's game privately, but woe betide the wretched man found doing so. Forest laws were made to prevent the stealing of game, and when poachers were caught, they were blinded or branded, or had their ears and fingers cut off, particularly their forefingers, which made it very difficult to pull a bow-string afterwards.

But though 'having lost their freedom the English were deeply afflicted', and though men hated William I, they certainly respected him, and many admired his strength and fearlessness. One Englishman who lived at court for a time and had watched him carefully wrote, 'King William was a very wise man and very powerful. He was mild to the good men who feared God, and over all measure severe to the men who gainsaid [contra-dicted] his will . . . so that no man dared oppose him. But it is not to be forgotten the good peace he made in this land so that a man might go over his realm unhurt with his bosom full of gold, and no man dared slay another.'

This useful state of things was a great triumph for William, but unfortunately it did not last long after his death in 1087. Then his lands and wealth were divided between his three sons, Robert, William, and Henry. Robert, the eldest, was an im-petuous but easy-going man, so soft-hearted that he even wept in sympathy with criminals who were brought before him for punishment. To him William I left his Norman lands, but his kind nature was not a great help to his subjects who would have preferred their duke to be strong and severe with law-breakers so that they might live in peace and security.

William, the second son, seems to have been his father's favourite, though he was not an attractive person. He was short, fat, and ungainly, with curious speckled eyes and a purple-red face, which gave him his nickname Rufus. When excited or angry he stuttered so badly that few could understand his speech. Like his father he was bold and ruthless, and like him, too, his greed was known to all men. Rufus became the king of England in 1087 and reigned till 1100, when he was mysteriously killed while hunting in the New Forest, shot by some unseen bow-man.

Both Robert and Rufus died without any children, and the youngest brother, Henry, added both Normandy and England to the £5,000 in silver which the Conqueror had left him. His death in 1135 was followed by a time of terrible confusion and horror for England. All powerful men were divided into two parties, one wanting to put Henry's daughter Matilda on the throne, and the other fighting to make her cousin, Stephen, the king. Many of Stephen's party believed that no woman was strong enough to rule, and others disliked Matilda who was cold and haughty. But on both sides were men who frankly enjoyed fighting as a sport, and who made themselves wealthy by robbing and murdering. The struggle lasted for nearly twenty years, and in the end the two parties made peace by agreeing that Stephen should reign as long as he lived and then Matilda's son, Henry Plantagenet, was to become the king of England.

HOMAGE TO WILLIAM I
The figures are reconstructed from the
Bayeux Tapestry

4. The Village, I

ONE of the first things to remember about this country during the centuries which are called the Middle Ages is, that it did not look at all the same as it does to-day. If you could have flown over part of it in the year 1250, say from Bristol to Lincoln, or London to Glasgow, taking air photographs, you would have been surprised both by what you saw for yourself and from the photographs when they were developed. No one, of course, would expect to see enormous towns, railways, or aerodromes, but you might easily think the countryside, the farms, and vil-

HEADPIECE. A villager outside his house. You can see the framework of timber and the spaces filled in with 'wattle and daub', that is, with woven twigs smeared with clay or earth. The domestic animals were almost as much at home in the house as the family. Life was lived much more out of doors than today and the house was chiefly a place for shelter and for sleep

lages, would look much as they do now, because things do not change so quickly in the country as they do elsewhere. Yet looking down on Britain in 1250 would be almost like looking on a foreign land, and you would probably be astonished at the shaggy, untidy wildness of it. The villages were tiny groups of houses with irregular patches of cleared land around them, some showing bare and brown, and others different shades of green and yellow according to the time of year and the state of the crops. Often great stretches of forest, far bigger than the woods we know to-day, surrounded these clearings, looking as if they were trying to shoulder them out of existence and blot out the narrow rough tracks which wound through the trees or linked one village with the next. The great forests of Britain have mostly disappeared now, though some of their names still remain, like the Forest of Arden, and of Elmet, and the Caledonian forest in Scotland, and the wild, untidy look of the land has gone too, and been replaced by the landscape we know of compact villages and neat fields, not very large and enclosed by walls or hedges.

In the village of the Middle Ages the houses clustered round the church, as indeed they still do to-day, for wherever you go you usually find the tower or spire poking up among the oldest houses in the place, and the same is also true of towns which have gradually grown up from villages. Try looking round your own town and see if you cannot find some ancient buildings, or perhaps the market-place, quite near the parish church. The church was then the centre of the small community, and very important. The building was used for the worship of God, for christenings and burial services, and so on, but also as a storehouse, sometimes as a prison, and, in times of danger, even as a fortress. The church bell, rung by the priest who lived close by, told men when to begin work, when to come home from the fields, and when to put their fires out and go to bed.

Normally there was one dwelling larger than the rest, often called the manor house or the grange. In some places the lord lived here all the year round, but in many he only came for occasional visits to see that all was going well, and to take possession of the dues that people owed him. This was because a rich man had other houses and estates in different parts of the country, and he spent his time travelling round from one to another, never settling anywhere for long. Sometimes he did not use the manor house at all, and the villagers never saw him. In these cases his manager or steward looked after the estate, and might live in the manor house himself. Occasionally in parts of the country which were very wild, where men were much given to raiding, carrying off cattle and hostages, and where life was generally perilous, the lord built himself a castle, and almost always his house was fortified, and, if possible, built of stone. All the other dwellings were very small, mere huts they would seem to us, not built close together in rows but each standing in its own small garden with perhaps a little bit of a field behind, called a croft. Fifty houses would be considered a very large village, and most had far fewer.

This cluster of buildings, church, manor house, and cottages, formed the centre of the place, and all round lay enormous unfenced fields, sometimes stretching as far as you could see. There were generally four of them, a great meadow for hay, and three others for growing food-crops, such as wheat and the 'oats and beans and barley' that you hear of in the folk-song. Only two out of these three were used each year, one lay fallow, that is, it rested and recovered some of its richness for the future. Fields can recover this without lying fallow, but then they must

Horses were too valuable to be used for ploughing; oxen were used instead

have plenty of manure, and of that there was very little in the Middle Ages. Besides these four fields there were sundry odd patches of rough grass or heath—the commons—where the cattle, geese, and sheep were put to graze until the haymaking in the meadow was over when they could be allowed on the meadow, and beyond the fields and commons lay woodland and waste, where firewood could be gathered and the pigs driven for acorns. In the village every man was a farmer, and obtained most of his food by the sweat of his own brow, and not by going to a shop and buying it. He did not then have all his land together as farmers do now, separate from other people's and surrounded by hedges and ditches, nor did it belong to him. Instead all the land belonged to the lord of the manor and lay in the four great fields. As the lord could not possibly use it all, he let out some of it to his villagers, keeping, of course, plenty for himself. The fields were divided up into strips of various shapes and sizes, as you can see in the picture on page 57, and each man held a number of these strips. It was quite usual for him to have up to sixty of them, and roughly speaking each one measured about half an acre, so that an average holding was thirty acres. Some of the poorer people had far less than this, perhaps only four or five acres. One man's strips did not all lie side by side, but here and there in different parts of each of the fields. The reason for this was that the fields were so big that the soil in them varied a good deal. Look at the east field in the picture for instance. Down by the stream it was rich and easily grew heavy crops, but across, towards the waste land, the soil was poor and stony. The only fair thing to do was to scatter men's strips, so that everyone had a share of good and bad land. Although there were no hedges between them, it was not very difficult to tell where one man's portion of land ended and another's began, because the ploughing was done in such a way that an extra deep furrow was made between them. Nowadays many fields still have what are called 'ridge and furrow' markings in them. They show very clearly in air photographs, and you can imagine each of these ridges belonging to a different person, and divided by the furrow from the next man's piec

The farmer in the Middle Ages could not choose for himself what crops to plant on his strips. Only in his garden and croft could he do as he liked. In the open fields he had to grow the same as his neighbours, and indeed all the ploughing, sowing, and harvesting was done at the same time. One year, for instance, the great north field of the village would be planted with wheat, the south with barley and beans, and the east would lie fallow. The haymaking, too, was done all together, each man cutting with his scythe his own portion, tossing and cocking it, and carrying it when dry. The lord sometimes had strips in the fields like everyone else, but often his were all put together round the manor house, and were always known as the demesne.

Obviously this method of strip-farming was very different from the modern way and it has almost entirely disappeared now in Britain, though it is still used in other parts of Europe. We hear more about it after the Norman Conquest, because people then began to keep more written records about land and farming, and this often makes one think that it was something new that the Conqueror brought with him. But the Normans did not invent it, though they used it at home. They found it here too when they came, and it was then very old. It had some great drawbacks, one of the worst was the waste of time spent in going from strip to strip, and another was the fact that if you happened to work next to a lazy farmer you suffered from his weeds. From time to time two men would see these drawbacks and would manage to come to a friendly agreement and exchange strips, so that they at least got a few of their sixty near together. In spite of difficulties the open-field method lasted in most places in Britain for hundreds of years. Only in very hilly or thickly wooded country it was never used. Here each man cleared and fenced his own little fields, for large ones were impossible.

Nowadays if you rent a farm, or even a field from someone, you go to him on quarter days and pay him so much money for the use of it. He gives you a receipt and that is all. In the Middle Ages men paid for their land quite differently. We saw that when William the Conqueror granted estates to his barons they did him homage and promised to give him service, military service, that is, to send or take a number of fully armed men to help him in time of war. They gave some money too, but the service was the most important thing. This sort of bargain—land for service—went on long after William's time, and was used between other people besides the king and his great tenants. In fact, a quite unimportant man who, as lord of a manor, let out land to his villagers, always demanded service in return, though not military service. Everyone who held strips of the lord, had to work for the lord on the demesne or about the manor house itself, the amount varying with the number of strips he held. About three days work a week was very common, which was a good deal when a man's own land had to be tended on the other three and all his food grown on it. All sorts of work had to be done too, anything in fact that the lord needed. A man had to be ready to plough at the proper time, either using his own plough if he had one, or the lord's if he had not. He might even have to draw it himself, but usually several villagers managed to make up a team of six oxen between them—for very few owned more than one—and guided the plough in turns. Horses were not much used, and oxen were more popular, partly because they did not need shoeing, and partly because, as a certain Walter of Henley wrote: 'When a horse is old and worn out there is nothing but his skin, but when an ox is old, with ten pennyworth of grass he is fit for the larder.' Fit, perhaps, but distinctly tough! Beside ploughing, sowing, harvesting, men also threshed the corn, helped the shepherd and swineherd, repaired the manor house, built barns, gathered apples for cider, in fact they turned their hands to any job on the land, and sometimes they were sent miles away to bring back a load of salt or stone, or of herrings for the lord's table. All the work was hard, and the hours were long. At Stoneleigh, in Warwickshire, reapers were expected to be in the harvest-field from sunrise to sunset, and even to eat their breakfast as they worked.

A MEDIEVAL VILLAGE

1. The forest
2. The old wooden castle on motte
3. The fields
4. The manor
5. The moat
6. The malthouse
7. The church
8. The tithe barn
9. The high road
10. The river
11. The villagers' huts
12. The Moot Place
13. The watermill
14. The windmill
15. The commons

But this week-work, as it was called, was not the end of the matter. At very busy times, like sheep-shearing, haymaking, and harvest-time, extra work had to be done, and this was called boon-work or love boon, because it was supposed to be done out of love for the lord. Really his tenants usually cursed him bitterly rather than loved him when, at the busiest moment of their own haymaking, they were called to do extra on the demesne. The only cheering part was that the lord was supposed to give good meals to everyone at love boons. For instance, at Stoneleigh men sat down to a hearty dinner at noon, each having 'a little wheat loaf, 4 eggs, and pottage, viz. Grewell without flesh boiled in it, cheese and beer'. At Brailes, also in Warwickshire, a certain Adam Underwood and his whole family, except his wife, had to go to the love boons at haymaking and harvest, and their lord gave them his second-best mutton and cheese to eat, and allowed them to take away the vat, in which the cheese was made, full of salt. A great deal of talk and argument must have gone on as to whether the cheese really was the second or only the third best. Beer made all the difference to men's feelings and to their work, but some lords were unpleasant enough to go in for dry boons and even hungry boons, and these were, as you can imagine, most unpopular.

Week-work and boon-work might seem quite enough for a man to give in exchange for his land, but there were other things as well. Often he had to give some of his own produce too, such as six bushels of oats in the autumn, a dozen eggs in the spring (Easter eggs in fact), and a fat hen at Christmas, and these were called dues. Then, too, when a man died, his heir had to give a heriot to the lord, which often meant the best cow, sheep, or pig, and he could not have the dead man's land unless he paid a tax called a relief, even if the land had been granted to the

DRY BOONS WERE ALWAYS UNPOPULAR

family for years and years. For everything the people of the village got they also had to give, whether it was permission to collect fuel from the woods, to feed their pigs on the waste, or to grind their corn at the lord's mill. Always the lord or his steward watched carefully to see that no man escaped paying for these things.

We have already noticed two peculiarities about life in the village, the open fields and the giving of services and dues in return for holding land. But there was another which, like these two, has now completely vanished. Today if anyone living in a village wants to move to another part of the country or to change his job, he is perfectly free to do so, provided he can find a house and another job to go to. In the Middle Ages very few people had the right to do this. Only the lord, who was obviously his own master, and certain others called freemen. Freemen did not have to labour on the demesne in return for holding land. Their service was much lighter, and consisted of such things as attending the court at the manor and riding about the fields with rods in their hands to see that other people worked hard. They paid a small sum of money to the lord each year, and were quite free to give up their land and move if they wanted to. There were never very many of them, however, and the majority of the villagers were in quite another class. They were called villeins, or, if they had very small houses and holdings of land, cottars, and the lord had them completely in his power. To begin with, a villein could not leave the village. If he ran away he was caught and brought back, and punished for trying to escape. He could not marry or let his sons and daughters marry without his lord's permission and, if he got it, he had to pay a sum of money called a merchet. He could not let his sons become priests if they wanted to without getting leave. The lord preferred to keep as many people as possible 'in villeinage', as it was called, because they had to stay in the village and work for him. If too many became free and could come and go and owed him no week-work, how was the demesne to be tilled? When once a man became a freeman, his family and descendants could never be villeins again. For a long time the only hope for a villein of becoming free was for him either to escape and remain hidden from his lord for a year and a day, which was not an easy thing to do when you could only travel on foot and you either had to take your family with you or leave them to starve; or else to persuade his lord to grant him freedom in exchange for a lump sum of money and a yearly due paid ever afterward. And it often took a man his whole lifetime to save enough for this. Villeins and cottars were indeed tied to the land, which may sound as if they were nothing more than slaves.

THRESHING CORN WITH FLAILS
About 1300

But it is important to remember that the land was also tied to them, and this had distinct advantages, for they were always sure of being able to earn a living from it. They had security, and it was not easy for the lord to turn them out. For one thing, he needed their work on his demesne, and he ate the eggs, cheese, and chickens which they paid him in dues, and warmed himself with the firewood they collected for him. For another, to treat a villein very badly would be to go right against the ancient custom of the land, which had been handed down from father to son for years, and which everyone, including the lord, knew and respected. So really villeins were not the same as slaves whose lives were controlled entirely by their owners. A villein's condition certainly depended a good deal on his lord's will, but it also depended on the custom of the land, which said that his house and strips should not be taken away nor his services and dues made unbearably heavy; and the lord could not treat him exactly as he liked, unless he was willing to take the consequence, that is, a village full of sullen resentful people being as difficult as possible in every way.

Gradually more and more men came to hate being villeins and longed passionately for complete freedom, and we shall see, as time went on, that they began to find more ways of escaping from villeinage, and that lords of the manor became more willing for them to do so.

APPENDIX TO CHAPTER 4

Adam Underwood of Brailes, Warwickshire, held thirty acres of his lord, the Earl of Warwick, and in return he had to give the following services and dues:

1. Work every other day except Saturday—from Michaelmas to Lammastide—that is, Monday, Wednesday, and Friday from October to August.
   Work two days a week from August to October.
   The work could be ploughing, haymaking, harvesting, carting stones (for walls and buildings), gathering nuts.
2. Work at love-boons at haysel and harvest.
3. Give dues of seven bushels of oats, a hen, food for three horses, three quarters of malt, twelve marks at Michaelmas, one penny for every pig over a year old, and a half-penny for younger ones.

He could not let his daughter marry or make his son a priest without leave.

5. The Village, II

THE largest dwelling in the village belonged to the lord of the manor, even though he might only live in it for a short time each year. Sometimes, as we have said, it was a castle which he had built for defence against ill-behaved neighbours or, if he lived near the Scottish border or the Welsh marches, against raiders who came to steal everything they could lay their hands on. Such castles were first built of wood and then, as time went on, of stone, and they stood on the highest ground near the village and often looked as if they were watching rather grimly over it and beyond to the country round. The remains of many of them, large and small, can still be seen, and sometimes the name Castle Hill in a village shows that once there was a stronghold there which for some reason has now disappeared.

Even if he did not build a castle, the lord always had a larger and better house than his tenants. This, too, was first of wood, but, like the castle, was replaced as soon as possible by a stone

HEADPIECE. Interior of villein's hut

house. It was not very large, and when the lord was at home so many people lived in it that it must have been very crowded and uncomfortable. There was one large room on the first floor called the hall, which was reached by an outside staircase, and the ground floor was used for storage and workshops. The hall went right up to the timbers of the roof and had small windows piercing very thick walls. It was a cold and draughty place, even when there were two fireplaces and when, as time went on, the walls were covered with tapestry. There was a kitchen leading off one end, and at the other a small private room for the owner and his family. The hall was by far the most important part of the manor house, for everyone lived and ate in it, and many servants slept there at night lying on the floor, which was covered with rushes or hay, and it was also the favourite sleeping-place for all the household animals. Here the lord held his court, which was an important meeting called to deal with the affairs of the village, to decide what work was to be done in the open fields, and to hear complaints and punish men for their misdeeds. Round the manor house lay a courtyard with stables and cow byres, and probably a large barn for storing corn and hay.

A few stone manor houses can still be seen, but the houses of the ordinary people of the village—the freemen, villeins, and the cottars—have quite disappeared. This is because they were such poor, and even flimsy, little places, and hardly ever built of stone even when it was plentiful. Most of them had a wooden framework, as you can see in the picture, and the gaps between the wood were filled in with walls of clay or mud rammed down hard, or by long pliable twigs woven in and out and then daubed over with mud. The mud was mixed up with bits of straw or hair to make it stick together, and some men were so skilful at

PAYING DUES

All the figures are based on pictures in the Luttrell Psalter

laying it on the twigs that they were given the nickname of dauber by their neighbours, which often stuck to them as a surname. The help of a John Carpenter and a Roger Dauber would be in great demand by villagers who could not, or would not, build their own houses! Thick walls of this kind were pretty strong and kept the inside of the house dry; but if they were thin or the wooden framework feeble, the house could actually be pushed over by a few strong men, and in the winter the driving rain would come through and make the inside uncomfortably damp. The roof was thatched with straw or reeds, perhaps by a man nicknamed thatcher, and the eaves projected well beyond the walls to keep the rain from softening them. Inside the house was rather dark and distinctly smelly. The only light came from the door when it stood open, and from very small windows without any glass in them. Glass was rare and very expensive in those days and so was only used in churches, by the king, and wealthy lords and merchants, and even they often took their windows about with them when they travelled from one of their houses to the next and used them everywhere they stayed. Other people closed the 'wind's-eye' with a shutter of wood or plaited twigs which kept out the light and the air.

The house was very smoky because the fire usually burned in the safest place, which was on a stone or iron plate in the middle of the earthen floor and away from the walls, and there was no chimney. The smoke got out as best it could through the door or window, or through a hole in the thatched roof, and in the winter when the door was shut, and the wind blew the smoke back through this hole, the inside of the house was 'ful sooty' and people coughed and rubbed their bleary eyes because of 'the smoke and smolder'.

Besides this the house must have had an unpleasant smell, partly because in those days people washed very little, and partly because they had a habit of keeping their livestock in their houses. Some hens would certainly be scratching about on the floor, or laying eggs in the corners, and a pig or two might spend the night under the table. No wonder that Geoffrey Chaucer, a poet who lived in the Middle Ages, said people were often much annoyed at night by 'the hungry fleas that frisked so fresh'. However, we must always remember that they were quite used to these hardships and took them as natural, and indeed there are many thousands still living in the same conditions to-day in backward countries of the world.

The house was rough and poor, and its owners lived hard, rough lives. They had very little furniture, only a wooden table, a few stools, and a chest to keep their clothes in, all made by the family in their spare moments. They had some cooking-pots, and ladles, and wooden bowls, and they used wooden spoons and fingers to eat with. Round the walls, instead of pictures, hung some of their tools, and perhaps a home-made basket or two, and dangling from the rafters there would be bunches of dried herbs and onions, and a precious ham or a side of bacon. Sometimes the whole family, hens, pigs, dogs, and all, lived and slept in one room, but sometimes the house had a second chamber leading off the living-room. Here the humans slept, lying on bags of straw on the earthen floor, and covered by coarse rugs made by the women and girls. Pillows, if they had any at all, were made of straw too, or else were nothing but good round logs of wood. At night their only light came from spluttering home-made candles, which were so precious that most people went to bed as soon as it was dark. In many places the church bell rang at sunset to remind them to look to their hearths and lights for fear of fire breaking out.

Sunrise was the time when most villagers began to stir and set about their day's work. They were busy all the year round, since they not only grew their food, but also made nearly everything they wore and used, from shirts and shoes to stools, spoons, harness for the oxen, and toys for the children. In the spring the men worked hard at the ploughing of their strips in the fields, and sowed the corn and harrowed the earth to cover the seed. They put a temporary fence round the meadow to keep the animals from grazing in the growing hay, weeded the strips, and looked after the lambs and young pigs which were arriving. Each family dug and planted their own garden with onions and leeks, cabbage and parsley. The summer brought sheep-shearing and then haymaking, and was a very busy time when there was a great deal to do, and when the lord was in the habit of demanding love-boons, wet, dry, or hungry. Then came the harvest, and it is difficult for us to imagine how important was the gathering of the wheat and oats and beans and barley, which had to provide most of the food and drink of the village through the year. No wonder that the carrying of the last sheaf was the signal for great rejoicing. Everyone took a holiday and a harvest-home feast was given by the lord. The entire village went to this and ate and drank as much as they could, and afterwards sang and danced, if they could stagger to their feet.

After the harvest-home, when autumn came on fast and days grew short and the air began to have a cold nip in it, people were busy preparing for the winter. All the corn had to be threshed by hand, which was a long business, the grain being beaten from the stalks with a tool called a flail. The men had to plough one of the three fields and sow winter corn, they had to thatch the ricks, and mend their roofs as well as the lord's. Wood and turf for fires were cut, nuts gathered, and the old sheep and cattle were killed off and the meat salted down and dried for the winter. Often it did not keep at all well and had to be cooked with many spices to hide the strong unpleasant taste. There was plenty of work for everyone, and quite small children acted as swineherds and drove the pigs into the woods to eat the acorns and beechnuts which fattened them up before they were killed and turned into bacon. Winter, of course, was a hard time. The houses were at their dampest and most draughty, and sometimes, after a poor harvest, or when a mur-rain had killed off some of the beasts, food became very short. If you read an account of meals provided by the lord during harvest boon-work or at Christmas feasts, the food sounds quite good, and certainly there was plenty of it—wheat loaves, four eggs each, two sorts of meat such as pork or venison, dishes of

THE MANOR COURT

herrings or pike, as well as unlimited cheese and pottage. At these times the tables must have been loaded with good things and with such drinks as cider and spiced ale, but everyday food was probably rather monotonous even when it was spiced with cinnamon and cloves, or flavoured with parsley and garlic. Breakfast was usually a hunk of brownish bread and a drink of sour ale, and dinner the same with perhaps some cheese and an onion. Supper was the main meal of the day for most people, and then they might have hot pottage, bacon, or a rabbit poached from the lord's wood. But often there must have been nothing to eat but sour bread made of 'beans and peases', a few curds and cream, and some 'last night's cabbage', which sounds distinctly unpleasant.

Most of these special feasts were held in the hall at the manor house, or in the big barn. One table was raised a little higher than the others and here the lord and his family sat, if they were at home. If not the steward occupied the chief seat, with the priest next to him, and then the freemen, and then the villeins with the largest holdings of land, and so on down to the poorest cottars and their skinny families, all with enormous appetites.

The whole village knew the hall well, not only because of the festivities which went on in it, but also because the manor court usually met there. In some places this was held about once a month, in others three or four times a year. The lord or his steward took the chair, and the freemen had to attend, for it was their chief service. Other villagers came when they were ordered to. When the lord was seated and everything was ready there was a single loud shout of 'oyez'—from the French word meaning 'listen'—and silence fell upon the meeting. Some-times, for specially important and serious matters, everyone in

RABBITING WITH A FERRET AND NET
This method of catching rabbits is still used

the village over twelve years of age had to come, and then the meeting was called the court leet and 'oyez' was shouted three times before the business began. Part of the business of the court had to do with the village farming; there, for instance, it was decided when to start ploughing, and when to turn the animals off the meadow and begin to grow the hay, and every man had to work his strips according to these plans. Then there was always a good deal of discussion about services. For instance, the steward might complain that a certain villein John, nicknamed Merrygo, because he was a cheerful soul if rather idle, had scamped his week-work, left the demesne at noon, and tried to persuade other men to go too, and that he ought to be fined. John, who had been ordered to appear in court, might say that he was only supposed to work till noon, and that the amount of ploughing he had been given to do was too much to do in the time. This was the sort of case which the lord, if he were wise, asked the freemen about, and if they declared that by ancient custom week-work always finished at noon, then no punishment was given. If, however, they thought the villein was wrong, he was fined and the lord took the money. It was to the manor court that a man came when his father died, and as the heir he wanted to take over the land. Since everyone in the village knew everyone else, it was usually easy for the court to decide who was the rightful heir to the dead man in case of any dispute. When this was done the new holder of the land, before he could take possession of it, was obliged to give his best beast to the lord as a heriot, which was a death duty out of the property which had come to him. Naturally people were always reluctant to part with the finest cow or sheep, and it was probably often a case of offering the poorest one dared. Here also came any unhappy villein who, without permission, had arranged a marriage for his daughter, or tried to smuggle his son into a nearby monastery to be trained as a priest and so to slip through the door to freedom. In one such case his lord, who was actually the abbot of the monastery, made the father buy the boy's freedom by saying the whole of the psalms ten times over for the soul of the late abbot and paying a fine of ten shillings! And if any man had been grievously insulted or injured by another, perhaps by being called villein when he was free, by being attacked and beaten in the dark one night, or by having his growing crops mysteriously trampled down, he came to the manor court to put his case and claim redress and his lord's protection. Of course in all these cases the lord, being the most powerful person present, had the last word, and, if he was unjust and cruel, that word could be terribly oppressive to his tenants. Obviously, too, it was useless, and might even be dangerous, to accuse him of wrongdoing, but if the tenants of such a man could seldom win a case against him, at least they had the right to claim a fair hearing and protection against others, either their equals, or even neighbouring lords, and the force of public opinion could make even the worst of lords think twice before bullying someone badly.

In spite of all the strenuous work, the poverty, and the dangers of living under a harsh and unjust lord, life in the village was by no means unbearably hard and miserable. For one thing people did not work all the time. There were a great many holy-days, probably about fifty in the year, when no one did any work or at least not after noon, and roughly speaking this gave everybody one day off in the week as well as Sundays. The great festivals of the Church, Christmas, Easter, and Whitsuntide meant a week or a fortnight free from services on the demesne, and at these times people found plenty of ways of amusing themselves. Feasts have already been mentioned, and of these perhaps the Christmas celebrations were specially popular, for the good food and drink, the steaming wassail bowl, and the warm fire in the hall made a cheerful relief in the cold dark days of winter. Then the villagers roared with laughter at the antics of the mummers in the Christmas plays, and they danced to well-known carol tunes, perhaps singing such words as:

> Make we merry more and less
> For now is the time of Christmas.
> Let no man come into this hall,
> But that some sport he bring withal,
> And if he say he cannot sing,
> Some other sport then let him bring,
> That it may please at this feasting,
> For now is the time of Christmas.

Or they might take part in the old dispute between the holly and the ivy in which boys and girls always took sides.

In the summer there were games and dancing, and visits to the nearest fair to marvel at the tumblers and jugglers, and to gape at the cock-fighting and the performing bear. At all seasons, too, there were the ale-drinkings which were held at weddings and funerals, or to raise money for the church, and many a quiet bit of poaching went on especially in the season of summer when the air was soft and the woods green, and the waters so beautiful and so bright that a great desire to catch a fish might come over a man as he wandered beside them. It is impossible not to sympathize with one culprit who, when he was summoned to the manor court for poaching, said to his

JUGGLERS AND AN ACROBAT

There was a great deal of time to spare in the medieval castle, and wandering entertainers of all kinds, singers, harpers, jugglers, and acrobats were always welcome

lord: 'Sir, for God's sake do not take it ill of me if I tell thee the truth, how I went the other evening along the bank of this pond and looked at the fish which were playing in the water, and, for the great desire I had for a tench, I laid me down on the bank and just with my hands quite simply and without any other device I caught that tench and carried it off.' Unfortunately, the end of this case is not told, but we hope the lord did not take it too ill!

6. Henry II restores Order

THE bargain made between Stephen and the haughty Matilda in 1153 put Henry II on the throne of England in 1154. This young foreigner—for he was a thorough Frenchman and though he could read English never learnt to speak more than a few words of it—was twenty-one when he was crowned, and was the first of a long line of fourteen kings, called the Plantagenets from the gay yellow broom flower that was in their family arms. Their reigns occupied a period of over three hundred years, and many very important things happened during that time. They were a mixed lot, weak and strong, wise and foolish, and Henry II was one of the strongest and most interesting of them. For-

HEADPIECE. Henry II. The first Plantagenet to rule in England. The broom plant from which the name comes is over the king's right shoulder

tunately for us, the people that knew him at the time found him interesting too, and some of them wrote descriptions of him. For instance, one of the king's chaplains, by name Peter of Blois, who wrote some letters about the court, described his master. Peter said that Henry was a strong broad-shouldered man, with a thick neck and long arms, his dark red hair closely cut, and his powerful legs rather bowed from much riding on horseback. We know, too, that he dressed untidily, that his hands were seldom clean, and that his watchful grey eyes missed little that went on around him. Nothing could tire this energetic king. He loved hunting and would ride all day through the woods and marshes until his legs were sore and blistered, and even then would not sit down quietly and rest, but would walk about and eat his supper standing up, which was most trying for his attendants, who could not sit while the king was on his feet. If he sat down, his hands would be busy with pen and paper, or a piece of hunting gear, his mind with problems of money or law, and his tongue with talk. He seemed able to do several things at the same time and to do them well. This restlessness and energy made him a difficult master to serve, especially as he often changed his plans with lightning speed.

He travelled frequently from one of his houses to another, as all great men did in those days, and one of his more annoying habits was making sudden plans to start very early in the morning. This always put the whole court in a turmoil, servants and squires packed and loaded baggage on to horses, and collected valuables, and dogs, and hawks; for moving a great household was a tremendous business and meant taking everything, clothes, bedding, hangings for the walls, and even windows, as well as supplies of food, weapons, armour, and harness. After hours of confusion and hard work everything would be more or less

ready, and then as likely as not Henry would keep his whole
court waiting because he had woken up late, or had become
absorbed in eating, or talking to his lawyers. Soon it would be
too late to start out on a long journey, or the king would
change his mind completely and decide to stay where he was,
and then everything had to be unpacked again by hungry, tired
servants. No wonder some men detested this way of living, and
one of them wrote: 'I often wonder how anyone can endure the
annoyances of court life. There is no order, no plan and . . .
moreover the bread is like lead and unbaked, the wine often
sour and mouldy, and the beer is horrid to taste and filthy to
look at.'

But Henry, though he often seemed careless of men's time,
did not waste his own, and though he spent much of it in hunting
and travelling he did many other things besides. He was a very
well-educated man in our modern sense of the word, for he
could read and write, and he loved books, which was quite
uncommon at a time when it was not thought at all strange if a
great man was unable to sign his own name. Henry was seldom
without a book somewhere near at hand, he read at meals, and
he read in his council, and when he was not reading he was
talking to every kind of person, but specially to lawyers and
learned men. His mind was always on the alert, and he never
forgot a face even if he had only seen it once. It is said that he
understood every language spoken between the French sea and
the Jordan river, though he only spoke French and Latin.

Like many others of his family he had a shocking temper,
and when anything angered him he would roll about on the
floor, biting the straw and his own nails in passion, and sobbing
and shouting aloud. In these black moods no one dared to cross
him, and he would often say things which he never meant at all.

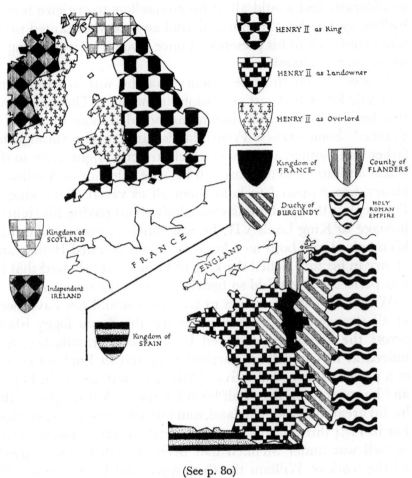

HENRY II as King

HENRY II as Landowner

HENRY II as Overlord

Kingdom of FRANCE

County of FLANDERS

Duchy of BURGUNDY

HOLY ROMAN EMPIRE

Kingdom of SCOTLAND

Independent IRELAND

Kingdom of SPAIN

FRANCE

ENGLAND

(See p. 80)

But, in spite of such terrible rages, the king could be mild and considerate, and would allow his counsellors to criticize him to his face and without resenting it, and anyone who wanted to see him could go into his presence at once, even if he was dining or in his private chamber.

It was a good thing for Henry that he was so strong and energetic for he had vast possessions to manage. The map shows that besides England his dominions included more than half of France.[1] Some of these French lands came to him through his father and mother, and others which stretched right down to the warm and sunny south, through his wife, Eleanor of Aquitaine. Henry was supposed to hold them all as vassal of the king of France, but though he was scrupulous about paying his rightful homage to King Louis VII, he was much more powerful than his overlord and both men knew it. Louis detested Henry, and Henry in his turn defied the king of France, and showed that he was perfectly able to do so because he was the stronger.

With such vast territories to control it would not have been at all strange if Henry had neglected the damp foggy island across the Channel conquered by his great-grandfather, and indeed at first he felt no particular interest in England except as a place to draw wealth from. His heart was always in France and he spent more than half his reign there. Yet in spite of this he did great things for England, and not before they were needed. For in 1154 this country was in a wretched state. Twenty years of civil war under Stephen had been enough to undo nearly all the work of William the Conqueror and his two sons. No chronicler was now able to say that it was possible for a man to go unhurt through the length of the land with his breast full of gold, for many people were too terrified to go anywhere. The

[1] See p. 79.

barons had learned to do exactly as they liked, feared no man, and obeyed no law, for no one was strong enough to control them, and Stephen had needed their help far too badly to dare to annoy them. They built themselves castles without permission, and when they were not fighting officially for Stephen or against him they rode forth with armed men to terrorize the countryside, burning towns and villages, and driving off cattle, and ruining the crops. Men dared not resist for fear of being flung into the castle dungeon and tortured. The description of the tortures are terrible to read, for prisoners were hung up by the feet and smoked with foul smoke, or by the thumbs with burning brands about their feet, or they were forced into chests too small to hold them with sharp stones to crush their limbs. The wretched people passed their days in fear and anguish, eating raw roots and the flesh of dogs, for men scarcely dared to till the ground, and harvests rotted in the fields. No wonder the chronicler reports that 'Corn, flesh and cheese there was none in the land and men said openly that Christ and his saints slept'. The need for a strong man to restore peace and order was desperate, and that man was Henry II.

He first set to work to destroy the castles which had been built by robber barons. Those that were of wood were comparatively easy to pull down and burn, but the stone ones were a greater problem, and if their owners refused to obey him Henry had to send armies against some of them. No one could defy the king for long, however, because he had all the power and wealth of his French lands behind him. He sent home all the foreigners who had come to England to help Stephen, among them a terrible set of robbers nicknamed the Flemish Wolves.

Henry was determined to make all men, rich and poor, respect the law of the land. The barons liked to try people accused of crime in their own courts because they could make money by the fines inflicted, or by seizing the property of the guilty ones. But Henry wanted money himself and he probably wanted people to be tried more fairly than they were when the local barons were the judges. So he forbade the barons to try anyone accused of serious crimes like murder, and instead sent out his own chosen judges to travel round from place to place through all the shires of England and hear these cases.[1] These judges, being the king's men, were interested in carrying out his orders to give the people justice, and not at all in trying to please the barons. Gradually more and more people realized that trials before the king's judges were much fairer than those held in other courts and were perfectly willing to go long distances to appear there, and gradually, too, the country became safer and more orderly.

Henry knew very well that he might need an army to help him in his work, and that he might not be able to trust the barons to raise one for him. So in 1181 he ordered that men of every rank, from baron down to the ordinary freemen of the villages and the simple worker of the town, must keep weapons and armour ready for the king's service in time of need. Each man must have what he could afford to buy, from full armour for the rich to a padded coat and a spear for the humble, and it must never be sold but passed down from father to son. No one dared turn up with an old scythe blade or a rusty axe, for if he did he was severely punished, and might even lose a hand or an eye.

Henry II chose many shrewd and able men as judges, sheriffs, and ministers to help in the work of restoring law and order in the land, and among them there was one man of whom he was

---

[1] See illustration on p. 87.

THE PENANCE AT CANTERBURY

Henry II, after walking barefoot through the streets to the cathedral, knelt before the High Altar and submitted to five strokes of the lash from every bishop and abbot present, and three from every monk. The monk holding the lash belongs to the Benedictine Order

particularly fond. This was Thomas à Becket, the son of a merchant, whose family had come from Normandy and settled in London. As a boy Becket had gone to school in London, but had spent his holidays in the country with a powerful baron called Richer, a friend of his father's, who taught the boy to ride, hunt, and hawk. Thomas, who was quick and clever and graceful, attracted the attention of the archbishop of Canterbury and went to live in his household. The many important men whom he met there were impressed by his quick mind and good manners, and the archbishop himself recommended him to the young King Henry who appointed him to the very important position of chancellor. The two became great friends, and Henry delighted in Becket's company as well as in his learning and shrewd advice. The pair must have made a great contrast to each other; the king, big, restless, untidy and carelessly dressed; and Becket, slight and graceful, with rich and elegant clothes, and a habit of washing in scented water, for although he was a priest he loved finery and good living. For eight years they toiled together for the well-being of England, Becket always ready to work for the king's will and pleasure. There was one thing that Henry was particularly anxious to change. William the Conqueror, as one of his Church reforms, set up special courts where all men in holy orders were to be judged rather than in the ordinary law courts. The Church courts never inflicted any very severe punishments such as long imprisonment or death, they merely degraded a guilty man, that is, reduced his rank in the Church, or at the worst, excommunicated him. Large numbers of men were tried in these courts who had only taken minor orders, they were doorkeepers or readers or holy-water clerks, and were not really priests at all, and among them were many bad characters. The comfortable knowledge that the ordinary law-court could not touch them, no matter what they did, made such men reckless, and their many deeds of violence were scarcely punished at all. Henry was anxious to change all this. He wanted the Church courts, if they found a man guilty of a very serious crime, to hand him over for the ordinary courts to punish, so that really serious offenders could not shelter behind the Church laws, claiming 'benefit of clergy' as it was called.

Now when Becket was working as chancellor he knew what was in the king's mind, and had discussed plans for such a reform with him, but in 1162 something happened to change Becket's attitude, and before long the two great friends had become most bitter enemies. The archbishop of Canterbury died, and Henry, believing that Becket would help him even more with his reforms, appointed him to the post, made him, in fact, the head of the Church in England. Becket warned the king that his loyalty to the Church would now have to come before his duty to the king, but Henry would not listen, for he was as obstinate as anyone could be, and simply did not believe that his friend would no longer support him in everything he wanted to do. But Becket knew that there were many clergy who thought that the servants of the Church should not be interfered with by the king. A bad king might do great harm if he was able to control them and give them orders. Also they said that if anyone in Holy Orders was degraded by a Church court and then handed over to the ordinary one for another trial he was in danger of being punished twice for the same crime, which was quite unfair.

Before very long there came signs of a change in the new archbishop's behaviour. Every day now he rose before daybreak and prayed for a long time, every night he read the Scriptures long after his household was asleep. Although exquisite and costly food was still served at his table for his guests and officials, Becket himself had only bread and water. His outer clothes were still remarkable for their splendour, but beneath them, unknown to everyone except his private chaplain and his servant Brun, he wore a coarse shirt made of goat's hair. Becket was always in deadly earnest about everything he undertook.

Henry, who had laughed at first at the new Thomas, soon began to fume with rage, for his royal wishes were disregarded and his orders challenged and disobeyed. In particular Becket stubbornly refused to help in the reform of the Church courts. Soon a violent quarrel broke out between the two men. It lasted off and on for eight years, and in 1164 the archbishop fled to France where he poured out floods of angry letters which much disturbed the peace of Europe. At last, in 1170, the matter was patched up and Becket returned to Canterbury, but sleeping dogs were not allowed to lie quiet. Among the many people who had always hated him were the de Brocs of Saltwood in Kent, who now began to insult the archbishop in every possible way. They seized his wine, hunted over his estates, and stole his hounds, until Becket lost his temper completely and excommunicated them. Henry II was at Bur-le-roi in France when he got the news of this, which seemed a fresh outbreak of the quarrel, for Becket had promised not to excommunicate any important man without the king's leave, and he at once fell into one of his terrible passions. He swore 'by God's eyes' that the archbishop was a traitor and shouted out 'Will none of these cowards rid me of this upstart priest?' Four knights among those who heard the cry determined to answer it in a way they thought the king would like. Secretly they left the court and in the cold December evening set off for England. They stayed a

THE KING'S JUSTICES ON CIRCUIT

The King's Justices still go on circuit, and something of the old ceremonial
is still retained

night with the hateful de Brocs, arrived at Canterbury on 29
December, and marching into the archbishop's presence, they
ordered him to lift the excommunication. He refused and they
withdrew. Then Becket was persuaded by his attendants to go
into the great cathedral church for safety, but in the growing
darkness the four knights who had gone into the garden to arm
themselves followed him and tried to drag him outside. When
they could not they struck him down and slew him in the house
of God itself.

This black deed struck horror into men's hearts. Everyone
blamed Henry and waited for punishment to fall on him, for
they were sure that evil must come of it. For a time it really
seemed that this was so. Henry's sons rebelled against him,

some of his angry barons, glad of a chance to attack their masterful overlord, rose in the north of England, and the king of Scotland declared war on him. Becket was proclaimed a saint and martyr, and people flocked to his tomb at Canterbury to pray. At last the king decided to visit the tomb himself and publicly show his sorrow and repentance. Through the muddy crowded streets of Canterbury he walked alone to the cathedral, barefooted and dressed only in his shirt and a rough cloak, and there he knelt and prayed and confessed his guilt, receiving on his bare back five strokes of the whip from each of the clergy present. After spending the whole night alone in the crypt of the cathedral he returned to London, where he fell ill of a fever for several days, which is not altogether surprising. While he lay there sick and troubled, a messenger arrived at the palace with news that the king of Scotland had been defeated and lay a captive, and within a few weeks his sons and their ally, the king of France, also made peace, while the rebellious barons soon came to heel. It seemed as if a miracle had happened. No wonder that everyone believed that Henry's confession at Canterbury had brought him forgiveness and help, and that more people than ever visited the tomb of the blessed Thomas and prayed there.

Henry was never in quite such difficulties again as he was immediately after Becket's death, but he did not manage to reform the Church courts although many of his subjects thought he was right in trying to. The 'benefit of clergy', that is, the right of all men in Holy Orders to be tried in Church courts where very severe punishments could not be given, was not abolished till 1827, six hundred years after Henry II's death, though Henry VIII whittled it down so that great criminals and murderers were not allowed to claim it.

Many of Henry's worst troubles came from his four sons. The young Plantagenets, Henry, Geoffrey, Richard, and John, were a turbulent collection, and their father did not seem to know how to deal with them. He alternately bullied and spoiled them, gave them part of his vast lands, but allowed them little real power. All of them were restless and born for many men's undoing, and constantly rebelled against their father. Two of them, Richard and John, outlived him, and each in turn became king of England.

THE COURT OF HENRY II PREPARES TO MOVE
Based on figures in the Harleian MSS.

7. The Church, I

THE PRIEST, HIS PARISH AND WORK

A VERY important person in village and town was the parish priest, and he had a position not quite the same as the modern clergyman or minister has now. For one thing there were then no chapels or meeting-houses. Everyone belonged to one universal Christian Church whose head was the Pope at Rome, and went to the same kind of services, so that only the parish church was necessary. There would be one in each village but more in the towns as they grew bigger. This was true not only of England, Scotland, and Wales, but of all Christian countries. If you travelled in France or Germany or Italy you would find the same kind of services going on in parish churches and the

HEADPIECE. The church was the centre of village life. Village meetings often took place in it and the churchyard was sometimes used as a market

parish priest taking them, and everywhere, too, the language he used would be Latin, the universal language of the Christian Church.

Religion was then more important than anything else for most people. Their lives, as we have seen, were not nearly as comfortable as ours are, and usually a great deal more dangerous and frightening. There were no doctors, no ambulances, and very few hospitals. If you fell seriously ill you usually died, and while you were ill you lived with your family, who looked after you as well as they could. Sometimes famine or war came to the villages, and then many died at once, so that people were always wondering what life was for, and thinking about death too, and what would happen to them after it. To these problems the Christian Church gave them the answer. Before they became Christians the people had believed in and feared many gods, most of them cruel ones. But as Christians they were taught that there was only one God, that He was merciful and good, and that He had sent His Son to live on earth as a man to show people what God was like and to found the Church, which continued throughout the ages carrying on the work that Christ began. They thought it was important to be good because that was what God had made them for, and also because what happened to them after death, whether they went happily to heaven or miserably to hell, depended partly on whether they had led a good or a bad life. At the same time, the Church taught them that however bad they had been, God, through the Church, could and did forgive them if they were sorry. Very few people could read, and so they had to learn all these things through the Church which taught them in its services, through its priests, and through pictures—pictures painted on the church walls, pictures in coloured glass in church windows, pictures carved in stone on the outsides and insides of buildings.

The church was the centre of the village. Everyone was baptized and married in it, and they met there for services on Sundays and saints' days, and when they died they were buried close by in the churchyard. They used both church and churchyard for meetings, for celebrations, and sometimes even for plays. In fact it is true to say that the Church, which was able to teach them the things they most wanted to know, was also the home of most of their activities apart from their daily work.

The parish priest had to see that his people came to church, and he took all the services. But as these were in Latin and very few understood them word for word, they had to be taught the general meaning so that they could follow what went on, especially in the Mass, the most important service of all. The priest taught them the Lord's Prayer, the Creed, and the Ten Commandments, and he told them the stories of the Old Testament, and of the life of Christ and the holy saints. More than this, a good parish priest urged people to be honest and kind, and reverent in church, and to obey their masters. In other words he seemed to be able to help them in trouble and perplexity, and, since he was the only person who could, he was naturally important and had great influence in every village and town.

The priest's work did not stop at taking services and teaching. The sick and old and the very poor were specially his care if he, too, was to follow the teaching of Christ, and he had to try and help them, and to urge their neighbours to do so. Travellers went to his house for food and shelter, unless there was a nearby monastery where they could get hospitality. If there was one they went there, for the monks would give much better food and drink, and probably a softer bed than the parish priest could, for he was seldom a rich man. As well as all this he usually had to be something of a farmer and work on the land, for in return for his priestly duties he was given strips in the open fields like everyone else, and his share of hay and pasture, and this land was called the glebe. Of course he was a freeman and owed no work on the demesne, his service was looking after men's souls. Besides growing food on his glebe land, he had three other ways of getting his living. He had the right to take tithe from everyone in the parish, that is one-tenth of a man's produce each year, the tenth sheaf of corn and cock of hay, the tenth lamb born or chicken hatched, and a tenth part of honey and cheese, and nuts and eggs, and 'all that is dug with the foot', which probably meant garden vegetables. In towns he took one-tenth of all that a craftsman or a merchant produced and sold both in shops and markets. Then he also took some of the fees paid for special services, such as marriages and burials, and when the head of any family died and the lord had taken a heriot, the priest stepped in and claimed the second best beast, or tool, or suit of clothes as a mortuary, a payment which poor people naturally grudged, as it frequently meant they were left with almost nothing.

The parish priest lived close to his church, usually in a small cottage, like those in which most of his people lived, though sometimes he had a better house, more like the manor, with a hall, a kitchen, and a private room, and some farm buildings around, including a tithe barn, and you can guess what he stored in that. He was supposed to go soberly and quietly dressed, not too smart but not too shabby, and never in gay garments of more than one colour. Moreover, his hair had to be correctly cut as a sign of his profession, and shaved off on the

THE VILLAGE PRIEST TAKING TITHE

Some tithes still survive to remind us that the Church was once entitled to a
tenth part of everything the farmer produced (see p. 93). Mid-thirteenth to
fifteenth centuries

top and round the nape of his neck and over his ears, so as to
leave a circle of hair all round.

If the clergy did their duty properly they were very busy men,
taking services and caring for the church and everything in it,
helping the poor and needy, entertaining weary travellers, perhaps working on the glebe land and collecting their tithes.
There was certainly plenty to do every day, besides urging
people to lead better lives and reproving those who got drunk
and fought, or beat their wives, or stayed away from Mass.
Many parish priests were hardworking and devoted men—
Chaucer describes one of these in his *Canterbury Tales*—but
sometimes they were far from satisfactory, and set a poor
example to the people they were supposed to lead and help.

A PRIEST VISITING A SICK MAN

This must be a wealthy house because of the well-made table and bed

The parishes of England were divided into groups, and in charge of each group, which was called a diocese, was the bishop. He had to care for clergy and people under him and he had a number of duties which none but he could perform. He consecrated churches, ordained priests, confirmed children, and he drew attention to the faults of clergy and people, and if necessary punished them in his court, for in such a great body as the Church it was impossible to expect everyone to lead good lives. Often his diocese was so enormous that the bishop could not possibly visit every parish in it and then an archdeacon went instead, and acted as 'the bishop's eye' and held an inquiry into the behaviour both of the priest and the people. He would question four chosen men of the parish about the state of the church building, the books, candlesticks, vestments, and so forth, and also about the conduct of the priest. From the records of such visits we learn a great deal about the state of the Church. Sometimes the witnesses say that their priest is a good man and preaches well, sometimes that he is old and getting past his work, but often the tale they tell is a darker one. We hear of churches so badly kept that rain fell upon the altar and the walls were thick with cobwebs, and of priests who wore gaudy clothes, and spent their time hunting and drinking to the great neglect of their duties. The people complain that services are not held at all, or are gabbled through without meaning or reverence. Even in the great cathedrals the clergy often behaved very badly. At Exeter, according to one report, they laughed and giggled during the solemn services, and those, who sat in the upper seats of the choir stalls and had candles within reach, threw the drippings of hot wax on the heads of those below them with the purpose of exciting their laughter or silent hatred.

The clergy in their turn had complaints to make about their people. They, too, spoke of bad behaviour in church, and re-ported men for working on holy days, and for drunkenness and riotous living. They said that markets were sometimes held in the very churchyard itself, so that graves were trampled on and the Holy Acre defaced, and that at the church-ales, which were feasts held by the parish to raise money for the upkeep of the church, the people behaved scandalously, and wild games and unseemly dances went on. The archdeacon would listen care-fully and then either himself order the guilty ones to be punished, or, in very serious cases, send them to be judged in the bishop's court. The women who persistently did their washing on Sun-day might be beaten with a hank of linen yarn, a London inn-keeper who said in public that the sight of a priest made him feel sick was heavily fined, and erring priests were corrected and punished.

Bad clergy indeed there certainly were, irreverent men who lived evil lives, but for every one of these there were hundreds more who were devout and good, and hundreds of parish priests were like the one Chaucer chose to describe, who was learned and holy and lived a simple life serving his people. His parish was large and the houses far apart, but he would visit the very farthest one in all weathers if there was sickness or trouble in it. Often such men were of humble birth and understood perfectly the daily lives of their parishioners, their work, their difficulties, their love of merriment and feasting, their simple faith in God and His Son. Never haughty, or hard of heart or speech, he would not press his poorer people to pay their tithes, preferring to deny himself rather than see them in want. In short not only did he preach the Word of God to men but also followed it himself, and there were countless good priests like him throughout the length and breadth of England.

The parish church, then, was the centre of men's lives, and most important. Even if it was very small it had two parts to it. One was the nave, the body of the church, and this was for the congregation. There were no seats in the nave, as there are now, only a few stone benches round the sides, and people were supposed to stand or kneel through the services. Many of them lolled against the pillars or squatted on the floor, and we cannot blame them for it, though the priests naturally disliked such irreverence. The service was taken in the chancel—the priest's part of the church—and this was often raised a little higher than the nave, so that all might see what was going on. The whole building lay from east to west and had a porch on the south side, which was used for meetings. People were married

NORMAN

③

④

⑤

Lancet Window

EARLY
ENGLISH

⑥

②

Patterns

'Magnificent' Arch and Piers

⑦

Triple Lancet Window.

⑧

Clustered
Piers and
Arch

①

Plain Arch
and Piers

⑪

Capital

⑫

Doorway

DECORATED

⑨

⑩

Window

⑬

Window

PERPENDICULAR

⑭

there too, probably because it was a fairly public place and the ceremony could be seen by passers by. This was often important because in those days no written record of weddings was kept as it is now, and if doubt ever arose as to whether a man and woman had actually been married there were usually some onlookers who could declare that they had seen their wedding.

Just inside the church near the door was the font. It contained holy water, used again and again for baptisms, and it was kept locked, for people were apt to steal the water to make magic potions or to charm away ill health and misfortunes. You can nearly always tell one of these medieval fonts because it will have the marks on the rim where the lid was fastened down and locked.

There are four chief kinds of architecture used in English churches in the Middle Ages, and it is fairly simple to tell them apart.

Norman from 1066 to about 1200—eleventh and twelfth centuries.

Early English from 1200 to about 1300—thirteenth century.

Decorated from 1300 to about 1400—fourteenth century.

Perpendicular from 1400 to about 1550—fifteenth and sixteenth centuries.

A Norman church looks strong and solid, the walls are very thick, and the windows small, and so the inside is rather dark. The roof is held up by massive round pillars and the arches over the doors and windows are round, sometimes very plain and simple as in Fig. 1, sometimes much more magnificent as in Fig. 2. The craftsmen who built these churches, whether in towns or tiny villages, decorated the arches, the tops of the pillars, and the fonts with patterns cut in the stone. They particularly liked a zigzag pattern called a chevron, another called dog tooth, and others which looked like thick twisted rope, or a series of stars or simple flowers. Sometimes they carved rows of wonderful and amusing heads, cats and owls and dragons and even people too. If a Norman church had a tower it was square and solid-looking and usually not very tall.

As the years went on men became keener than ever on church building. They kept on trying new ideas and so new kinds of architecture grew. In the thirteenth century there was a positive outburst of enthusiasm with wonderful results, for some of our greatest cathedrals were built then as well as countless parish churches. These thirteenth-century planners and builders were also fond of enlarging churches by adding side aisles or wings to them, not always because more room was needed for the congregation, in fact the result was often a building far too large for the parish to fill, but because they delighted in making God's house as fine and beautiful as possible, and put all their skill and strength into the work. Early English churches are less solid and heavy looking than Norman ones. The windows are larger and the roof higher, and instead of single round pillars there are clusters of much thinner ones grouped in a solid bunch round a central or master-pillar. Arches are pointed, not round. Sometimes the windows are single and slender, and shaped at the top like the head of a spear, and are called lancet windows (Fig. 5). They give a good deal of light, especially if they are set fairly close together in the walls, and before long builders realized that they looked particularly fine if they were grouped in twos or threes with a little projecting ridge of stone above them. The ridge is known as a drip-stone and it is useful to throw off the wet away from the windows. If you look at Fig. 7 you can see how this grouping might be done. In the same window there are blank squares of stone above the shorter

CHURCH ROOF BOSSES

lancets which look rather flat and dull. It occurred to thoughtful
men that such blanks could be pierced with small openings of
various shapes and sizes, as in the windows in figs. 10 and 13, which
not only let more light into the church but also made beautiful
and exciting patterns, known as tracery. Builders became very
interested in tracery and they also filled the windows with
coloured glass through which the sun shone and made the inside of the church glow with richness. They loved, too, to
decorate the tops of pillars with carvings of foliage, sometimes
with small animals lurking among the leaves, and they planted
delicate stone pinnacles on the stalwart Norman towers.

It is the great increase of ornament which really gives the
name Decorated to the third kind of architecture in our list.
We have so far noticed arches, pillars, and windows, and watched
them for important changes, but now there are no completely
new features to remember. Arches are still pointed, pillars much

the same as in the Early English churches. But windows are
still getting bigger, and the tracery in their tops becoming more
and more complicated. In fact many a craftsman trying to fit
glass into the strangely shaped openings in the stonework must
have been almost in despair about the job. Besides this there is
far more decoration everywhere, round pillars and doors, on
pinnacles, and openings for water-pipes, and a great variety of
decoration too, oak- and rose- and vine-leaves, figures of animals
and men, and beautiful heads of kings and queens, knights and
saints, and some more homely looking faces which very likely
the carver copied from those of his mates.

The insides of churches became steadily lighter as time went
on, and bigger and bigger windows were made. In a Perpendicular church they have become so large that sometimes it seems
as if the walls were almost made of glass instead of stone. The
great churches of East Anglia, Gloucestershire, and Somerset
are magnificent examples in which the daylight is as clear inside as out. Perpendicular arches are no longer so pointed, in
fact they look as if they had been slightly flattened by some
heavy weight squashing them from the top, and they often have
square drip-stones framing them, as you can see in Fig. 12.
Pillars are not so thick as before because they have less weight
to carry. But it is in the windows that you can see most clearly
why this kind of architecture is called Perpendicular, because if
you look carefully at them they give the impression of straight
upright lines, not only in the stone strips dividing the lower parts,
but also in the tracery where larger straight-sided openings have
replaced the complicated small ones (Fig. 13). The glaziers must
have been much pleased by the change, and other craftsmen
copied the idea and used the new panel shape to decorate walls
and doors.

If you go into churches or cathedrals today you often do not notice much colour inside except on the altar, and sometimes on statues. In the Middle Ages it was very different. Then most churches were aglow with colour. Far more windows were filled with stained glass, and the walls were covered with pictures painted in rich reds, blues, and gold. A church was a cheerful satisfying building to enter, often the only one where men might enjoy the warmth and brightness of colour. And besides merely gazing at the figures of saints and angels, of Jonah and the whale, and of Tobias and his fish, they also learned many stories of the Bible, and saw vivid pictures of the heaven and hell which interested them so much. In fact a man might very well say:

> A painted paradise in church I see
> Where amid harps and lights the blessed dwell,
> And lost souls burning in a painted hell.
> Fearful is one, the other fair to me.

Christo Duce

8. Lion Heart and Lackland

Cœur de Lion—what a magnificent nickname to be given and to keep. Richard I of England is not by any means the only man who has been described by poets and storytellers as having a lion's heart, but he is the only one who is known to the world for ever as 'The Lion Heart'. It conjures up a picture of someone fierce, brave, and strong, and Richard was all these things, but he won his title to them far away from England and in the winning did little good to this country.

His father, Henry II, died in 1189, and two months later Richard came to London for his coronation. Most of his subjects then saw him for the first time, for he had already spent many years in France, but they must have been delighted with

HEADPIECE. Richard I. At top left, his seal; at top right, his helm; at bottom, his badge and motto what they saw. A greater contrast to Henry can hardly be imagined. Instead of the heavy bulk of that restless powerful old man with his red face and untidy clothes, they saw a splendid figure, tall and straight, and towering above his courtiers, a handsome face and thick tawny hair. He rode a splendid horse, too, specially chosen to carry his great frame, and he looked gay and cheerful. Unlike Henry he took care of his appearance and liked fine clothes. On one occasion he wore a tunic of rose-coloured samite, with a beautiful mantle embroidered with silver suns and half moons about his shoulders, and a scarlet cap on his head. A sword with a hilt of gold was fastened by his side, and bright spurs of gold to his heels. He had a red saddle studded with stars and bearing two lion cubs in gold at the back. He must have looked as handsome and strong as a lion himself. By 1189 there were already many stories told in France and England of his bravery in battle, and his mighty strength. But though his English subjects were to hear still more wonderful stories about him during the ten years of his reign, they were to see very little of their new king. For he was even then pledged to go to Palestine with the emperor of Germany and the king of France to fight a crusade against the Saracens, and as soon as he was crowned he began his preparations. The first thing was to raise money, money for ships, wages, and weapons, and as he set about this some people must have realized that he was not much interested in England for itself, but only as a source of wealth to be poured out for his favourite occupation of fighting. Richard seemed ready to do almost anything for money. Royal lands were sold off, royal officials had to pay high prices to the king to keep their jobs, and also to resign from them if they wished to do so, taxes were raised from everyone who did not join the crusade in person.

'I would sell the city of London', said Richard, 'if only I could find a buyer.' Every town in the country had to supply four horses, and every royal manor two for the king's use, many of them no doubt specially picked as good enough to be his personal chargers—and this demand for money was only the first of many that the Lion Heart was to make.

At last, when all was ready, Richard left his kingdom in charge of William Longchamp, Bishop of Ely, and crossed to France where he met King Philip Augustus, and they set off together for the first part of their journey. But they soon separated again, and Richard, with his men and horses packed in one hundred ships, sailed for Palestine from the port of Marseilles, while Philip marched on to Genoa. Careful rules had been drawn up by the king to keep order among his soldiers and seamen, and some of them sound exceedingly strict, to say the least of it. If one man slew another, he was to be bound to the body and flung into the sea at once without a trial. If any man gave but a blow with his fist, he was to be plunged several times over his head and ears in the water, and for theft, or pickery as it was called, his head was to be shaved, daubed with hot pitch, and then covered with feathers so that all might know him for a thief. Richard had certainly meant to keep order, but he was also a generous master, and all the seamen were paid a year's wages in advance.

This was the third crusade which had set out from Europe for Palestine. Twice before, in 1095 and 1147, Christian princes, knights, and humble people too, had answered the call of the Church, and taken up arms to free the Holy Land. For over five hundred years non-Christian people had ruled in Bethlehem and Nazareth and Jerusalem, people called Saracens, who were followers, not of Christ, but of the prophet Mohammed and the

SALADIN AND SARACENS

The crusaders probably copied the fine chain mail of the Saracens, because it was light and flexible, and comparatively cool

god Allah whom he preached. The Saracens were fierce and warlike, and determined to spread their religion by the sword, and though at times they allowed pilgrims to visit the holy places in the land where Christ had lived and worked, they more often prevented them, tortured, and killed them, or sold them in the great slave-markets of Baghdad and Damascus. Many Christians longed passionately to stop this, and wanted Palestine to be in the hands of those who worshipped their God and His Son, Jesus Christ, who had lived His earthly life in that country. And so in 1095 the first great army had collected, full of wild enthusiasm for the task. The soldiers in it put the sign of the cross upon their clothes and called themselves crusaders or soldiers of the cross. Most of them felt certain that it was a holy thing to fight in such a cause, but of course some went because they hoped for adventure and plunder, and above all for some delightful fighting in a righteous war. But whatever the reason, from far and wide men flocked to join in the crusade from castle and cottage, village and town, leaving behind their homes and all things dear to them. The writer William of Malmesbury said that the Welshman left his fighting, the Scot his vermin, the Dane his drinking parties, and the Norwegian his raw fish to fight the Saracens. He does not mention the English, although many of them went on all the crusades, but as he was an Englishman himself he probably expected his readers to know this.

At first the Christian armies had been successful. They conquered much of the beautiful land of Palestine, captured Jerusalem, and set a Christian king over the city. But the success did not last long; by 1189 the Saracens, under a brave and brilliant leader called Saladin, were once more masters of the land, the prisons were full of Christian prisoners, the pilgrims once more forbidden to visit the holy places, and the third crusade was to be a great effort to break for ever the power of Saladin and his people.

Now the Saracens, although fierce and terrible in war, were not savages by any means. They were in fact, more civilized in some ways than their would-be conquerors. Many of them were men of great learning, and had studied history and mathematics —the word 'algebra' was first used by them—and astronomy, the science of the stars. They were skilful doctors and wrote books about diseases, like measles and small-pox, long before people in England knew anything about them. They were builders and farmers, and their craftsmen made the most beautiful silks and the finest swords in the world. Then, too, their religion meant a great deal to them. They learnt by heart long passages from their sacred book, the Koran, in the same way as we learn parts of the Bible, and they were exceedingly careful to pray five times every day, turning towards their holy city, which was called Mecca. They also felt they were fighting in a holy war and longed to drive the Christians out of Palestine and set up the Mohammedan religion far and wide. Saladin, their leader, was a curious mixture of cruelty and kindness. He could be courteous and gentle to a gallant or a helpless foe, and often released the Christian women and children captured in the fighting because he could not bear to see them weep. He sent fruit and snow to Richard Cœur de Lion, his deadly enemy, when the king was ill and longed for something to cool his fever. But he was quite ruthless in battle, and had sworn that until he died he would fight to drive the Christians out of his land.

Richard's voyage to Palestine was rather a leisurely affair.[1] He called at Sicily to extract a large sum owed him by the king and seized the island of Cyprus to punish its ruler who had dared to plunder some English ships. At last in June 1191 he reached Acre in Palestine to find that many crusaders had already arrived including Philip of France, and had begun a siege of the town. But they were in a poor way, suffering from shortage of food, swarms of flies and the sickness these caused, and also from the jealousy and quarrels of their leaders. The coming of Richard did not do much to end the quarrels, for he was fiery-tempered and proud, and he and Philip were at heart the deadliest of enemies, even if they outwardly patched up their differences from time to time. Always the matter of the English lands in France lay like a black shadow between them.

[1] See the illustration on p. 111.

And when both fell ill of a kind of malaria their tempers did not improve. At the same time the presence of the Lion Heart put new courage into the crusaders, and they were ready to follow wherever he led. He was famous, he was generous—he paid his knights four gold bezants a month while Philip only gave three—he was full of spirits, and his magnificent looks and size alone cheered everyone up. He was also quite simply and honestly devoted to the task of rescuing Jerusalem, the holy city of all Christendom, from the Saracens. Many were the stories of his bravery that went round the great camp outside the walls of Acre. Sometimes he was too daring, and one day he almost lost his life because of this. He had suddenly decided to ride some way into the country to fly his hawks, and set off unarmed and with only a few attendants. While they were busy with their sport a band of Saracens saw them, and before any of the party knew what was happening they were surrounded. Richard would certainly have been killed or captured if one of his knights with great courage had not cried out, 'Here I am— Richard of England', and dashed off on his horse to draw the Saracens after him in hot pursuit. We do not know what happened to this knight, but the king took the chance given and made for the camp and safety.

After a long siege Acre fell. Richard was very ill at the time and could not take part in the fighting. He had his bed carried as near as possible to the hottest part of the struggle and lay there tossing and fuming but always cheering on his men. But when the town surrendered the good name of the Lion Heart was much besmirched by the heartless massacre of many help-less prisoners.

Very soon after this success King Philip announced that he was going home. He had been so ill that he had lost most of

RICHARD LION HEART AND THE THIRD CRUSADE, 1190–4

1. Richard I and King Philip of France sail from Marseilles in 1190.
2. Richard quarrels with the King of Sicily and destroys Messina.
3. Richard attacks and conquers Cyprus. Philip leaves him.
4. Richard lands in Palestine in 1191. He takes Jaffa and Acre, but although he fights Saladin for two years he cannot take Jerusalem.
5. He sails for home; but
6. he is shipwrecked and made prisoner by the archduke of Austria.
7. He remains a prisoner until 1194 when he is ransomed; and
8. he returns to his kingdom in 1194.

his hair and some of his nails, and there were urgent matters to be settled in France. But perhaps the real reason was that at every turn he was completely outshone by the Lion Heart whom all men followed gladly, thinking it great glory to fight under him. Philip simply could not bear it. He was more intelligent than Richard, he had invented the most useful machines for hurling stones and dead dogs into Acre, but he was small, and physically weak, and not a natural fighter. When he had gone, Richard alone was left to lead the Christians, and with a smaller army to capture Jerusalem—if he could.

He never did. Hopefully he started on the long difficult march from Acre to the hills where the holy city lay. Slowly the crusading army moved on, tortured with hunger, thirst, and flies, troubled by Saladin's warriors who hovered round ready to attack any weak spot or straggling group, towards the goal that they were never to reach. Twice they got within a day's march of it, twice they were halted by the terrible difficulties of the journey and by the fact that Saladin's unbroken army lay in the hills around the city. Richard himself rode within sight of the walls of Jerusalem, but it is said that he held his shield before his eyes and would not look at the city for he knew in his heart he could not rescue it. Certain by now that the odds against them were too great he gave the order to return to Acre and there he made a truce with Saladin. There was to be a peace for three years, and the Christian armies were to withdraw from the whole of Palestine save only seven cities which Saladin gave into their keeping. And then Richard set out to return to England.

Everyone knows that the adventures of the Lion Heart did not end there. He made up his mind, rashly as usual, to travel home overland, and landed with a few attendants near the town of Ragusa in Dalmatia. But he was on the territory of enemies who hated him, and almost from the first was a hunted man. He was caught and shut up in prison, where he lay for thirteen months while his English and Norman subjects searched their pockets again to raise the huge ransom demanded. There were a good many people not very anxious to see him free, for Richard had made a number of enemies by his pride and arrogance. Two men tried hard to persuade his captors to keep him in prison. One was the foxy Philip of France and the other Richard's brother, the still more foxy John, who was by now ruling England and the French lands. It was Philip who, when he heard that the Lion Heart was out of prison, sent the simple message to John 'the Devil is free again'.

At last after four years adventuring Richard returned to England. But if his subjects hoped that he might settle down to a quiet and slightly less expensive life they were utterly mistaken. In a very few months he was off again, this time to fight Philip over the French lands, and he never came back. For five years more he fought his old enemy, sending constantly to England for more and more money. At last in 1199 he was shot by an enemy archer as, careless to the last, he rode without full armour too near to the wall of a besieged town. The wound became septic and he died. He cannot possibly be described as a wise or good king of England, but in spite of all his faults and neglect most people admired and even loved the Lion Heart.

Most people came to detest his brother John, nicknamed Lackland, who succeeded him, and who was as great a contrast to Richard as Richard had been to their father Henry II. John was a strange and complicated character, sufficiently interesting for Shakespeare to write a play about him nearly four hundred years later. To look at he was not nearly so impressive as the

Lion Heart though he dressed magnificently, appearing on one occasion in a tunic of white silk, a crimson cloak sewn with sapphires and pearls, and white gloves set with large jewels. He was short and rather plump and soft-looking, instead of hard and fit. Where Richard was generous John was extremely mean. When he stayed for three days at the monastery of St. Albans, the monks, for whom the royal visit had been a great expense, were all agog to know what kingly gift he would leave behind when he went. Imagine their feelings when he left thirteen pence and a cloth which his servants had actually borrowed from the abbey itself. Unlike the energetic Richard, John had moods when he was utterly lazy and slothful, and (sometimes) lay in bed for the whole day, though he could be vigorous enough at times. He was often deliberately cruel and treacherous, and exceedingly rude, but he was also amusing and clever, and capable of making masterly plans in war. Like many of his family, the 'Black Angevins', he had a vile temper. It was not long before he was in trouble, and indeed during his whole reign of seventeen years he was never out of it.

Richard, when he died, was fighting Philip Augustus of France for the French lands, and Philip's passionate desire to drive the king of England out of his country made him continue the war against John, even though they had been on friendly terms when the Lion Heart was alive. Philip took up the cause of Arthur, nephew to Richard and John, who had a claim to the lands in France, which many people thought was better than John's. After a furious march of a hundred miles in less than two days John captured his nephew and shut him up in a castle. Shortly afterwards the boy disappeared, some said murdered by John, or, at least so terrified of him, that he jumped from the battlements and was killed. After this many of John's French

THE SEALING OF MAGNA CARTA, 1215
(See p. 119)

subjects deserted him and went over to Philip, and the war went
so badly that at last only Gascony and Poitou out of all the vast
territories belonging to his father remained in English hands. And
these remained loyal because the Gascons had a most flourishing
wine trade with England and did not want to lose it, and also
because like so many men of their times they were sometimes
amazingly loyal even to the most unpleasant lords. It was this
failure to hold the French lands that gave John the scornful nickname of Lackland, and even the more scornful Soft-
sword.

John never gave up hope that he might one day win back his
lost lands and castles and knights, and he was always trying to
raise money to do it. He used every trick he could invent to fill

his treasury, and this made him hateful to his English subjects. The king had the right to raise certain money and dues from his tenants, just as a lord of the manor could from his. For instance, we saw that in the village when a man died his heir had to pay a heriot to his lord before he could take over his land. In just the same way the king's tenants, too, had to pay a certain sum called a relief. But John demanded such enormous ones that the wretched heirs would be very nearly ruined.

The barons and knights who held land from the king owed him military service for it—that is they promised to fight for him in time of need and to provide a certain number of armed men according to the size of their estates. If one of these military tenants died and his heir was a small boy, it was obviously impossible for him to stagger to the war bearing an immense sword and with a man's helmet wobbling on his head. He could not give military service until he grew up. So he became the king's ward, his estates were managed for him by the king, and he was brought up and trained as a knight, very likely at the royal court. Now John treated his wards most unfairly. He was so greedy for money that he screwed every penny out of their estates for himself, selling the cattle and sheep, the pigs and hens, and cutting down the woods so that the houses and barns could not be repaired. The fishponds were cleared and not restocked, and whole estates went to rack and ruin, and when the wards were old enough to take them over, they found a dreadful state of affairs, and in fact were often poor for the rest of their lives.

Again John had the right to demand a payment of money from military tenants instead of their service. This was called scutage, and was never supposed to be asked more than once a year. John demanded it every year and sometimes twice yearly.

All these things, and many that there is not room to mention here, made John very much disliked. As he grew steadily more unpopular he began to put foreigners, mostly hateful men, into the most important posts in his kingdom, instead of Englishmen. He made them sheriffs and judges, and they tried men very unfairly, and punished them by enormous fines, and even by seizing all the family belongings.

Englishmen endured all this for years, the barons because they feared the power of the king, for though he might be losing lands in France he was not weak in England, the common people because they had no one to speak for them.

At last John got so badly into trouble that the barons seized the opportunity and made a united stand against him. In 1206 he quarrelled with the Pope, the head of the Christian Church who lived in Rome, about a new archbishop of Canterbury. John wanted to give this most important post to one of his friends, but the Pope appointed a far wiser and better man, Stephen Langton by name. In spite of a fine present of four expensive rings sent by the Pope to soothe him, John refused to accept Langton. In order to make him obey, the Pope put England under an interdict. Now this was a serious matter for everyone. It meant that the church doors were locked, and no services were held, the bells hung silent in the belfries, dust lay thick upon the altars, and weeds sprang up in the churchyards. There could be no christenings or weddings in church, no one might be buried in holy ground. People must have felt terrified at being cut off from all the comfort and help of priests and services. John did not care, he merely seized as much of the lands and money of the Church as he was able to, saying that since the clergy were doing no work they should have no pay.

Then the Pope went a step farther. In 1209 he used the terrible power of excommunication, and pronounced John an outcast from the Church, a man whom no one need obey and who, if he died unforgiven, would go straight to hell. He also invited Philip of France to invade England and turn the evil fellow off his throne. At this John gave in. Knowing how greatly he was hated, he feared England might go the way of Normandy and Anjou. He accepted Stephen Langton, he promised to pay back the money he had taken from the clergy and monks, he even gave up his kingdom to the Pope and did him homage for it, promising to rule it as a faithful vassal. In 1213, after a silence of five and a half years, the interdict was lifted, the church doors opened, and men sighed with relief as they heard the bells once more ringing across the fields.

But by this time a strong party of Englishmen, including many very important barons, had decided not only that the king must make reforms but also what reforms he must make. Helped and encouraged by the Archbishop Langton they drew up a list of their demands and presented them to John. The things they wrote down were not new; they were the ancient customs of the realm, such as the Conqueror and every king after him had promised to keep to. The barons had no objection to a strong king, but they were determined that he should remember the rules and govern by them. It was just the same as when a lord's tenants in the manor court stuck out for the ancient customs of their forefathers, and refused to bear more dues and services. Now the king's tenants were doing the same to him. John was nearly beside himself with rage, but the barons, united and undismayed, gathered their armed knights and marched into London, forcing the king to flee to Windsor. Here he realized that for the present he must give way, and on a flat little island in the middle of the Thames, with the green meadows of Runnymede on either side, he met the chief rebels, and was handed the great roll of parchment on which their demands were written in Latin. In future John was not to ask for costly reliefs, or waste the lands of his wards. He was not to ask for scutage or any other payment from military tenants unless they first met in a council and consented. Foreign judges were to be dismissed, and only men who knew the law of the land were to try Englishmen. No freeman was to be punished either without a trial or fined so heavily that he was hopelessly ruined. This document of seventy-nine clauses was called the Great Charter, and the royal seal was solemnly fixed to it on 15 June 1215. As it was written in Latin it is often known by its Latin name 'Magna Carta'. Then royal clerks began to make copies of it to send throughout the country, so that all men might know what the king had promised. After seven hundred years there

KING JOHN

Heraldry was not yet an exact system, and King John's personal badge was the crescent and the flaming star

are still four of these copies existing, and if you send two shillings and sixpence to the British Museum you can buy a photograph of one of them.

John had no intention of keeping these promises if he could help it. That very year he collected an army to fight the barons, but before he could do so he fell ill after feasting greedily on peaches and new ale, and died. The Great Charter remained to be handed on to his successors.

9. The Church, II

MONKS, NUNS, AND FRIARS

THE parish priest who, as we have seen, lived and worked in the village or the town, and his superiors, the bishop and the archdeacon, were not the only people in the Middle Ages to devote their lives in a special way to the service of God. There were also the monks, the nuns, and the friars. But these were different from the ordinary clergy, because they cut themselves off far more from the everyday life of the world around them. They lived in special houses and obeyed certain strict rules which had first been drawn up for monks and nuns by St. Benedict of

HEADPIECE. Artist-monk glorifying a madonna. Nearly all the arts were under the control of the Church. There was a constant demand for images and paintings, &c., to make the Christian teaching clear to a public which could not read

Nursia, and again hundreds of years later for friars by St. Francis of Assisi.

Monks and nuns lived in buildings usually called monasteries, priories, or convents, and by the year A.D. 1300 there were many of these religious houses dotted about over England, Scotland, and Wales. But they were not by any means the first ones to be started, for the idea behind them was even then very old, and had spread to Europe from the East.

For centuries some Christians had felt obliged to withdraw from the world and give themselves wholly to prayer and to thought about God, making this the most important thing in their lives, and spending as little time as possible over eating, sleeping, dressing, and washing. They found they could not do this properly if they lived among other people, for the dangers and temptations of the world and the demands of their friends and relations distracted them far too much. They had to get away and live apart. At first, when a Christian felt like this, he simply went off into some lonely place and became a hermit, that is, he lived by himself, perhaps in a cave or a tiny hut, eating the roughest and poorest food, enduring great hardship, and spending every day, and part of the night, saying his prayers and thinking about God. Such hermits often lived utterly alone, but sometimes a few of them collected in a group and shared a small chapel which they built with their own hands. But even in these groups each man still spent most of his time alone, and behaved exactly as he thought best. By the fifth century A.D. there were solitary monks like these, or groups of them in many parts of Europe, including Ireland, England, Scotland, and Wales.

Then in the year A.D. 529 an Italian, named Benedict of Nursia (later St. Benedict), founded a monastery at Monte

Cassino, and drew up a new plan for Christians who wanted to live apart from the world. He had been a solitary monk himself, but he had come to believe that it would be far better for him and others like him to join together in a society or community, living in the same building under a chief monk called the abbot. Benedict set to work and drew up a list of rules which explained exactly how a society like this should work and manage itself, rules which were so sensible and wise that many communities of monks were formed whose members obeyed them. Because they followed the rules of St. Benedict they were called monks of the Benedictine order. The order spread rapidly and new branches were constantly being started. St. Augustine, who came to England in A.D. 597, was a member, and he founded the first Benedictine monastery in this country, at Canterbury. Later on other new orders came into being, such as Carthusians in 1084 and the Cistercians in 1098, but they all used St. Benedict's first scheme as their pattern.

The monastic orders, as they are called—Benedictines, Carthusians, Cistercians, and others—usually chose to build their community houses in remote and lonely places, so that, although the monks themselves now lived together, they were still set apart from the world. You can get a very good idea of the quiet and the loneliness of some of the monasteries if you visit their ruins to-day—places like Fountains Abbey in Yorkshire, Melrose in Scotland, and Llanthony in Wales. It is true that some like Durham and Glastonbury and St. Albans are now in the centre of a town, but you must remember that the monastery was probably there first, and that the town grew up later, because the place became a centre of trade and work. But, whether the neighbourhood remained lonely or became busy, inside the high encircling walls of the monastery the monks and

THE CONVENT KITCHEN
'Rissheaulx' are being cooked. See p. 128

nuns lived their own special kind of life, and very different it was from that of the men and women outside.

Some monasteries were large and stately, and some were small and homely. Some, especially the earliest, were built by the monks themselves, others, the bigger ones, by the finest craftsmen of the day with large gangs of labourers to help them, and in the very latest style of architecture. But they were all usually on the same pattern. The chief building was the church where the monks worshipped God both by day and by night. As you can see from the plan on page 127 it lay east and west, and on the south, the sunny side of it, was the cloister. This was a wide covered passage running round the four sides of a square patch of ground, called the garth, which was usually covered by grass. Because the cloister was protected by the church it was warm and sheltered, and the monks spent part of each day in it. They worked and walked there and also—but only at special times—they talked there. On one side of the cloister there was often a stone trough with running water, where everyone washed before going into the refectory, or dining-room, for meals. The refectory was very like the big hall in the manor house. It had wooden tables, wooden stools, and a pulpit from which a monk read aloud during meals. Close by, naturally, was the kitchen and store-room.

Grouped round or near the cloister were the other parts of the monastery—the chapter-house, where the abbot held meetings of the whole community to discuss the business, give orders, or reprimand ill-behaved monks—the parlour, where a fire was lit from 1 November to 15 March, most likely the only one in the whole place except for the kitchen, and where the monks went to warm themselves. Close to the church and with a stair-case leading into it was the dormitory, and here the monks slept in their clothes so that they were all ready to get up quickly for the night services. And not far away was the infirmary, often with a special chapel and kitchen of its own. Here the old and sick members of the order were cared for by a monk specially chosen because he was 'gentle and good-tempered, kind and pitiful to the sick', and here at regular intervals everyone came to be bled. This was thought good for their health, and probably many monks looked forward to it, for it usually meant spending two or three pleasant days in the infirmary doing no work and eating much more interesting food than they got in the refectory.

Besides all these, a big monastery had other buildings, the abbot's lodging, a bakehouse, a brewhouse, barns and stables, and, set rather apart from the rest, the guest-house. It was the duty of all monastic orders to give food and shelter to travellers, but their guests were usually kept away from the monks in case they should distract them with exciting tales of the world beyond the monastery walls and make them restless and ill content. They were not allowed in the inner buildings round the cloister, though the more important ones sometimes dined with the abbot. But, even if they could not wander anywhere they liked, visitors were very well looked after by a monk called the guest-master, and he was kept very busy if the monastery lay near an important high road. He had to receive all travellers and make them comfortable, see that the beds were clean, the rushes on the floor fresh and green, the food served in unbroken dishes, and that there were no spiders or cobwebs in the corners.

Every monk had to take three solemn vows before he could become a full member of his order, the vow of poverty—he might not possess anything of his own—the vow of chastity—he might not marry—the vow of obedience—he must obey the head of his monastery and the rules of the order. His chief business was the worship of God. Seven times between dawn and dusk the monks went into the church and held services, and once in the middle of the night, even in the bitter cold of winter they were woken by the dormitory bell and went by the night staircase into the church for half-an-hour or more. It was not an easy life for people who took it seriously. The first meal came at midday when everyone had been up and busy since dawn, and the second—though not all monasteries had two—about 5 o'clock in the evening. So the ringing of the refectory bell must have been a pleasant sound. In strict monasteries the food was very simple—bread, soup, and meat, with per-haps some fruit, and beer to drink. On fast days, which were Wednesdays and Fridays and the forty days of Lent, the monks

A MONASTERY

1. Church
2. Cloister
3. Chapter-house
4. Monks' refectory
5. Monks' dormitory
6. Kitchen
7. Warming-house
8. Lay-brothers' dormitory
9. Misericorde
10. Infirmary
11. Infirmary chapel
12. Infirmary kitchen
13. Abbot's house
14. Almonry
15. Barn
16. Guest-house
17. Cellar
18. Stables
19. Prison
20. Fish-pond
21. Well
22. Orchard

ate no meat, only fish and eggs, but on feast days they had wine and extra food, especially sweet things. The nuns in the convent of Barking always had special little cakes called rissheaulx to eat on Sundays, which were made of figs, dates, sugar, ginger, and saffron mixed together, put into a pastry case, and then 'fraide in oyle'. These were the forerunners of our rissoles. They must have been rather like mince-pies and just as popular, for one of the nuns carefully wrote out the recipe for them, and it exists to this very day.

Talking at meals was generally forbidden so the monks invented signs for such remarks as 'Please pass the salt' or 'I should like an apple'. We know of one monastery which drew up a table of one hundred and six signs for use at meal times. Anyone who wanted fish would 'wagge the hande displaied sidelynges in the manere of a fish-taill', and the sign for mustard was to hold the nose 'in the righte fiste and rubbe it'. One can imagine a kind of wild dumb-show going on in the refectory sometimes, which must have been far funnier and more distracting than any speech. When dinner was over, the monks went into the cloister for a short rest and were allowed to talk, and if they were beginners or novices they could play quiet games. After this they went to work until it was time for the evening service and bed. St. Benedict believed that idleness was 'an enemy of the soul', and no one in a monastery was allowed much free time, but there were of course plenty of monks and nuns who managed to be thoroughly idle in spite of rules. The work they did, or were supposed to do, varied a great deal. There was always the actual running of the monastery which kept a good many people busy. We have already seen, for instance, what the guest-master had to do, as well as the monk in charge of the infirmary. Then the church had to be looked after, as well as the kitchen. The

THE FRIARS (BOTH FRANCISCANS AND DOMINICANS)
carried the Church's teaching into the street and the market-place (see p. 131)

cellarer, who was in charge of food, was one of the busiest people in the whole place, and the almoner, who gave out food and money to the poor, was also busy. Some monks copied out books by hand, writing with their quill pens along carefully ruled lines and leaving blank spaces for capital letters. Then others drew in the capitals and painted them in beautiful glowing colours, cobalt, vermilion, and green. The most important letters were gilded, and in the loops were painted little pictures of saints and kings, or animals and flowers. The monks of the Cistercian order were skilful farmers. They cleared the land round the monastery of trees, drained it, and farmed it very cleverly, and they kept great flocks of sheep and sold the wool and hides to merchants.

E

But, whatever the work was, it was all centred on the monastery, and, indeed, the monks were not supposed to go outside without special permission. But as the centuries went on more and more of them did get out, and not always with very good reasons. Some were allowed to become clerks and chaplains in the households of great nobles or bishops. Others travelled far and wide on monastery business, for gradually the monastic orders became very rich, and the monks had to spend much time looking after their property. Although St. Benedict meant monks to be poor and therefore free of worldly cares, nothing could prevent the monasteries from getting rich. Men and women, believing so strongly as they did then in the importance of religion, loved to give gifts to churches and monasteries, land and money and jewels, and to leave their property to the monks when they died. Such a man was John Courtenay, who gave land and money to the Cistercian abbey at Forde in Dorset, and was buried in the church there in 1273. John believed firmly that the prayers of the monks at Forde would help him wherever he was. Once, when he was returning to England from a voyage, his ship was in great danger from a tempest, he alone of all the company on board would not despair and he said, 'Be not afraid but take courage. Let us endure for one hour more, and by that time my monks at Forde will be risen to their prayers and will intercede for me to the Lord so that no storms, nor winds, nor waves shall be able to shipwreck us.' And, as in truth the storm did shortly die down, John Courtenay 'was in great joy', and believed more firmly than ever in the wisdom of giving good gifts to the monks. Unfortunately the effect on many of them, and on the friars, too, as we shall see, was to make them far more concerned about their property than about the service of God. St. Benedict thought that monks had two great duties to perform, to pray and to work, but as time went on many of them became too busy to pray, and so rich that they kept servants to do the hard work for them.

Friars are sometimes confused with monks, which would displease them very much for they were rivals, and there was little love lost between them. The two main orders of friars were the Franciscans, or Grey Friars, founded by St. Francis of Assisi in A.D. 1212, and the Dominicans, or Black Friars, founded by the Spaniard Dominic in 1215, and they came to England in the thirteenth century, much later than the monks. Both orders were forbidden to own any property, and they begged shelter and food as they travelled from place to place. Like the monks they obeyed strict rules and took the three vows of poverty, chastity, and obedience. But where the monks withdrew from the world and lived mainly inside their monasteries, the friars went about everywhere, mixing with people, caring for the poor and sick in their own homes, preaching and teaching all and sundry in streets and market-places as well as churches. At first their simple, hard, and faithful lives were very like the pattern of their master Christ, and their preaching helped and comforted thousands of people. They did their greatest work in towns—where they deliberately chose to live in the worst quarters—'outside the city walls in a filthy swamp at Norwich, ... in a mere barn-like place with walls of mud at Shrewsbury'; in the 'Stinking Alley of London'. And in such places the friars began for the first time to cope with a new problem, the poor and sick, and the helpless who lived so wretchedly there and were ill cared for, because the towns and their populations were growing at such a tremendous rate. Their bare feet, their rough clothes, and the strange fact that at first they refused to accept any money caused a great stir wherever they went. The friars were never allowed to own property except the houses they lived in, and this was another way in which they were different from monks who, by the fifteenth century, owned a quarter of all the land of England. But unhappily the friars, too, became more and more interested in money and began to work much harder at their begging, especially in rich houses, than at their preaching and their care of the poor. So that by the end of the Middle Ages although there were still many lovable saintly people to be found in monasteries and friaries, there were also many who were greedy and lazy.

AN ILLUSTRATED CAPITAL M
showing the Virgin Mary carrying the Infant
Jesus to Egypt

10. The Town

THE picture above shows a little town in the south of France
from which, in 1249, the saintly Louis IX set sail for the Holy
Land on a crusade. It is called Aigues-Mortes and probably
looks today very much as it did six hundred years ago and
as many other towns looked in the Middle Ages, not only in
France but in England too. Most of them were surrounded by
strong walls, very like those you can see in the illustration,
though some relied for their safety on earthen ramparts topped
with stockades of wood, and some like Cambridge and Bristol,
were protected by a river and deep ditches, and some like
Chester by both. Inside the walls, houses, churches, and gardens lay huddled closely together but secure, and it was perfectly clear where the place began and ended, for there were no
straggling ugly suburbs sprawling far out from the centre, as in

many modern towns. Only gradually as life became more peaceful were houses built outside the protecting walls. These walls were kept in repair by the people of the town, the burgesses as they were called, and they were pierced by a number of gates—London had seven, and Coventry twelve—which were the only entrances. They were guarded by specially chosen gate-keepers who opened them at dawn and shut and locked them at sunset, and it was well to be in good time in the evening if you wanted to go in, for when once the great gates, made of solid oak with iron bars across the back, were closed it was impossible to get inside till morning, unless you were a person of the highest importance. During the day-time the burgesses passed in and out as they liked without any difficulty, many of them being known, at least by sight, to the gate-keepers, for medieval towns were very small compared with modern ones. A stranger, however, even if he came only from another town fifty miles away, was looked on as a foreigner, and would be questioned closely about his business before being admitted, and if he came with anything to sell in the market, he would certainly have to pay toll. The rougher people of the town were quick to notice strangers, and often bullied and baited them abominably. In 1421 the burgesses of Coventry were warned about their rude behaviour, and ordered not to throw things at 'no strange man, nor scorn him'!

Outside the town and coming close up to its walls lay the fields, so that the sights and sounds of the country were never very far away, and however hot and stuffy the streets might be in summer a man could still catch the musical rasping of a scythe being sharpened, and smell the sweet hay as it lay drying, and he could slip through the gates and see at once the fresh green of fields and woods. There were common pastures, and hay meadows, and big stretches of arable land divided into strips where the burgesses grew crops and fed their cattle and geese, for many of them were farmers as well as workers in other trades or crafts. Naturally as time went on a baker or weaver would find it less and less possible to do both things at once, and preferred to spend all his days working at his craft, and to rely on buying most of his food instead of growing it. But even then the busy seasons of the farming year, haysel and harvest, lambing time and ploughing, were well known to everyone and people took it as a matter of course that they should help to get in the crops even though they lived in a town.

Inside the walls, although the buildings were often closely packed, there were also a good many gardens as well as orchards and small crofts, where cattle and sheep could be pastured when they were brought in at sunset. It was a common sight to see farm animals being herded through the town, and sometimes they lived there. For instance, in the reign of Edward I (1272–1307) we find that Londoners were allowed to keep their pigs in their houses if they wanted to, though they might not let them wander at will in the streets. Usually a pig which was found straying in London was caught and killed as a nuisance, but if you met a pig with a bell around its neck you had to be careful to leave that one alone, for the bell meant that it belonged to the Hospital of St. Antony, whose pigs were allowed to wander about London and pick up what food they could, until the time came for them to be killed and eaten in the hospital. Coventry was much stricter than London. No swine at all or ducks were allowed to wander in the streets and there were to be no pigsties near them.

The streets of the town were narrow and winding, a few of them would be paved with cobble-stones, but most were simply earthy tracks. None were lighted at night except where a householder chose to hang a lantern in front of his door or where a tavern stood. There were many odd dark corners and backyards where evil-doers could lurk, ready to pounce on a late passer-by and rob or wound him. All towns were supposed to appoint armed watchmen to patrol the streets, who had the right to raise the 'hue and cry' (see p. 162), that is, to call on citizens to help chase suspicious characters with shouts and yells. But even so the back streets could be distinctly dangerous even in broad daylight. In any case many of these watchmen must have been like Master Dogberry and his followers, whom Shakespeare makes such fun of in his play *Much Ado about Nothing*.

The streets were also dirty, for people threw even more rubbish out of their houses and into the streets than they do today, and there were no regular dustmen with their carts to clear it. It lay rotting and smelly, unless the hospital pigs disposed of it, or people cleaned the road in front of their own houses. On very special occasions, such as a royal visit to the town, men called scavengers were set to clean the chief thoroughfares, but otherwise a good thunderstorm was the only hope. Yet, because the medieval town was still so close to the country and had still so many gardens, and orchards and open spaces within its walls, the danger and unpleasantness of smells and dirt were far less than people sometimes think, and the air was far fresher and more healthy than in many towns of today in spite of the fact that we often pride ourselves on our modern drains and water-supply.

On each side of the streets were the houses, some of them just like the simple little cottages of the village but others standing close together and much taller. They were usually built in the same way, too, with wooden frames and wattle and daub, and

FURNITURE IN A MERCHANT'S HOUSE
In this case Dick Whittington's. Mid-fourteenth century. (See p. 138)

thatched roofs. But fire was a far worse danger in the town than in the village, because the houses were closer together, and so gradually stone and brick foundations became common, and tiles or wooden shingles were used for roofs. And as soon as people moved their hearths from the centre of a room to one of the side walls, they had to learn how to build safe chimneys of stone.

Many houses had two or three floors, and the upper stories projected out beyond the ground floor which made the downstairs rooms rather dark especially in the narrower streets. The townspeople liked to walk along under the overhanging part to avoid being hit by things thrown out of a top window. Often with no more than a sudden shout, which sounded like 'Gardy loo', buckets were emptied into the street and the unhappy

passer-by was drenched with dirty water. The cry meant
'Look out, Water' and was a careless way of saying *Gardez-
l'eau*.

If the owner of the house was a merchant or tradesman, he
had his shop in the front on the ground floor. Generally it was
a work-room as well, so that the customer could see the goods
actually being made before being hung out round the open
window and the door, much as boots and poultry and such
things are hung to-day. Behind the shop was the kitchen, the
storehouse, and the brewhouse, a shed or two, and, no doubt,
the pigsties. The owner and his family lived up above, in rooms
which had little furniture in them, but which, if they were
prosperous people, gradually became more comfortable. A
wealthy burgess probably had glass in his windows quite as
soon as the baron in his castle, and by the end of the fifteenth
century the rooms were often hung with tapestry or painted
cloth, or panelled in oak which made them 'warm and much
more close'. The furniture was simple; heavy plain wooden
tables and stools or forms, with perhaps a carved chair for the
master of the house, and a chest for keeping clothes in. A prosperous family would eat and drink from pewter plates and mugs,
and very likely own a silver salt-cellar and a handsome silver
cup. The food of a poor townsman would be as simple as that
of a poor villein in the country, but people of the richer sort in
towns had a great variety of eatables. In London, along the
river bank where the cook-shops lay, you could buy every kind
of fish, flesh, and fowl, roast meat, baked meat, stews, and
pasties, besides rich spiced pies, marzipan, gingerbread, and a
great assortment of wines. In 1445 a good goose cost fourpence
in the midlands and a pig's head a penny.

Nowadays in towns the shops are scattered about, so that a

STREET SCENE IN A MEDIEVAL TOWN

butcher may be next to a baker and a grocer alongside a fish-monger, but in the Middle Ages each trade kept to its own district, so that corn was for sale on Cornhill, meat in Butcher's Rows, tailors worked in Threadneedle Street, and so on. Only the taverns lay here and there among them, easily recognized in the day-time because a bush of fresh green leaves would hang outside whenever new ale was in stock, and at night by the lanterns which innkeepers were made to light. The town was always full of bustle, and the burgesses were busy men, especially if they were still partly farmers as well as craftsmen and had to till their own land. Now the land had to be paid for and, as we know, the commonest way of paying was by doing service for the lord of the manor, be he the king, or abbot, or knight. But how impossible it would be for a busy weaver or saddler to carry on his craft if he was obliged to work three days a week for his lord, to say nothing of extra love-boons as well. Somehow townsmen had to get free of services, and bit by bit they managed to make a bargain with their lord by which they promised to pay him money instead. These bargains were carefully written down as they were made and sealed. They were called charters and might be won from the king, or a baron, or the abbot of a neighbouring monastery, or whoever the owner of the town lands might be, and if for some reason he was in need of money he granted the charter more readily. Richard Cœur de Lion and John both granted charters when they needed money for the crusade or the war in France. John, in fact, granted over seventy.

Usually the monasteries were the most unwilling to grant any charters, and from them the burgesses screwed their rights bit by bit. For instance, the burgesses of Bury St. Edmunds got a charter from the abbot in the thirteenth century by which they each paid twopence a year for every acre of their land instead of week work, and escaped from harvest-boon by another penny an acre, and from fetching cartloads of eels from Southrey, twenty miles away, by yet another penny. But still each man was compelled to do some part of the ploughing on the abbot's demesne, so that they were not freed completely by their first bargain. Gradually, however, all townsmen were released from service in exchange for money payments.

There were two other things that the burgesses of the medieval towns wanted specially besides their freedom from service to the lord. They wanted the right to manage their own affairs, which meant choosing their own officials and not being under his steward. And they wanted to hold their own court to try men who broke the rules and customs of the town, instead of having to appear in the manor court. Gradually, as the years went by, they won these rights, so that in time all burgesses were free men, and they met once a year to choose their own town council of twelve or twenty-four men with one chief burgess as chairman. He was sometimes called the mayor, sometimes the provost or bailiff, and he and the council made the town laws and punished those who disobeyed them. They also collected from the burgesses the rent for the lord of the manor and handed it over in a lump sum.

The town was never dull, the streets were full of bustle and noise, and colour. Village people, when they came on a visit, must often have been quite envious, not only because the burgesses seemed freer than they were, but also because life seemed so full of excitement. A man like William Merrygo for instance, that cheerful sociable fellow, loved it all. The only time he really did any service without a single grumble was when he went to fetch a load of salted herrings from the market-town twenty miles away. He was fascinated by the sight and sounds —the noise of apprentice boys shouting their wares 'Come buy, come buy, my masters' they cried; 'New shoes', 'Hot pies', 'Fine new brooms'—the grand appearance of the mayor in his official robe of scarlet, tipped with fur, as he walked to a meeting of the town council. William stared at the market-stalls and goggled at the juggler, standing near the gateway throwing balls into the air and catching them with marvellous skill, while his assistant stood on his head, or walked along on his hands. With a groan he would drag himself away to fetch the salted herrings which his lord was to eat on fast days or in Lent. He got them from Simon Winterflood, the master fishmonger, who lived near the river. Simon was one of the chief men of the town and a member of an important society called the Fishmongers' Guild. In a medieval town there were a number of these guilds, usually one for every trade. The butchers, the weavers, the hatters, the tailors all liked to have their own, because it helped them to manage their trade as they thought proper.

Simon was a power in the fishmongers' guild. He employed several men and had three lively apprentices. They were the most junior members of the guild and they were bound to work for their master for seven years. During that time they lived in his house behind the shop and he promised to teach them all about fishmongering. They learned to catch eels, pike, and salmon in the season, to know the best places for mussels and lampreys, and to look after the lines, and nets, and wicker eel-traps. They had to be able to salt fish down in barrels, for this was always in demand. People ate fish on every Wednesday and Friday in Lent and on certain other fast days by order of the Church, and, of course, it was impossible to get it fresh in inland places. The apprentices very much disliked the job of

MYSTERY PLAY

Good, Evil, and Death assemble backstage. Note also the Hand of God

salting, for it made their hands raw and painful, but they had to do it for it was so profitable. As well as teaching the apprentices the mysteries of the fish trade, Simon gave them food, clothes both of linen and wool, and shoes, and he beat them soundly when they scamped their work or ran off in work hours to play football in the streets! After seven years the apprentices moved up into the next rank of the guild and became workers paid by the day. Then they were called journeymen—from the French *journée*, meaning day—and were free to change their master if they wanted, and even to pack up and look for work in another town. A journeyman could move up into the most important rank in the guild and become a master craftsman, but first he had to do two things. He had to produce a masterpiece of his work, good enough to reach the high standard set by the guild, and he had to be able to pay a subscription—sometimes quite a heavy one—into the guild fund. Often very skilled men could not afford this and remained journeymen all their lives. This meant that they could never have their own shops or take apprentices.

The guilds always tried to keep up the standard of work in the trade, and to see that the customer was charged a fair price for what he bought. Bad or hastily made goods were forbidden, and there were strict rules to be kept. The guild members appointed 'searchers' to go round and see that all was well. The searchers of the fishmongers often sniffed round Simon Winterflood's shop on the look-out for stale fish. They tested his scales and weights in case he was giving short measure to customers, and if he was caught doing so he was punished. But a good tradesman usually welcomed the searchers, for he knew he was protected by the guild in many ways. For one thing no non-guildsman could sell or buy in the town without paying a heavy toll, and so many 'foreigners' were kept away and trade was reserved for the townsmen. For another, if a member fell on bad times, through illness or accident, he and his wife and family would get help from the guild funds, and if a man died his funeral was paid for, his widow helped, and often his sons apprenticed without any fee. There was the comfortable thought, too, that the guild paid a priest to say mass for the souls of departed members, there were excellent feasts arranged on special occasions, and there were the guild plays. The whole population turned out to watch these and people flocked in from neighbouring villages. They took place in the summer when the days were fine and long, for they were performed in the open air. Scenes from the Bible, from the story of the crea-

tion of the world to the life and death of Christ, were acted by
the different guilds of the town, and they were very popular.
Everyone had a good chance of seeing them, for the actors performed on big wagons especially decorated, which were called
'pageants', drawn by horses round the different places in the
town. Sometimes the plays were performed in the churchyard,
sometimes in the church itself, for the clergy had often organized
them before the guilds took them over. No one thought it in the
least strange to see plays being acted in church, even quite
noisy and funny ones, because, although the most important
things about the church were the services which went on there,
it was also the centre for nearly all the sociable gatherings of
a parish, and everyone felt quite at home there. Behind each
pageant marched the guildsmen who were to act, with cloaks

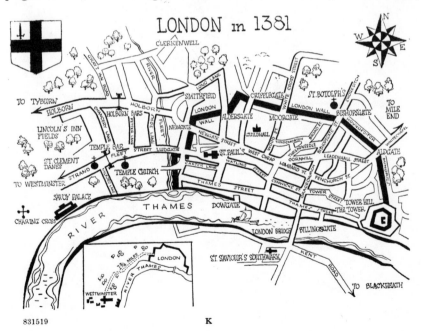

LONDON in 1381

drawn closely round them to hide their costumes. When the pageant stopped they climbed up on to it and started their play. Simon Winterflood was delighted when the fishmongers were given the scene of Jonah and the whale to act. It seemed so suitable, and besides it could be made very funny indeed, and the onlookers always liked a good laugh, though they would watch the play showing the birth of the baby Christ reverently and quietly. What with paying the members who took part, and buying the clothes, and rigging up the pageants, the guild paid out a good deal of money for the plays, but everyone thought it well worth while, especially the apprentices, who loved a holiday, and the innkeepers, for their ale was much needed by the thirsty audiences who stood so long in dusty streets and hot sun to watch the whole round of plays.

11. Trade and Travel

THE town was always busy, but on market-day, which was usually once a week, the noise and bustle were tremendous. For this was the day when people from the country round about came in to sell their surplus produce and to buy the townsmen's goods. The sounds of hammering and banging and shouting started early in the morning as the stalls were put up in the market-place, which was in any open space near the centre of the town. The king's permission was necessary before a market could be held, unless it was a town custom so ancient that it was before the memory of man. This permission might be granted to the town council or to the lord of the manor, whoever he was,

HEADPIECE. The pillory. A twin model of this one is preserved at Coleshill, Warwickshire and it was a very valuable thing to have because a great deal of money could be made through it, and for this reason men were ready to pay a good deal of money to the king for his permission. First of all, the market owner took a toll on everything brought in for sale. At Bakewell market in Derbyshire in Edward III's reign if anyone brought a cartload of goods he paid a penny, on a horseload he paid a halfpenny, and on a man-load a farthing, and, though this sounds very little to us, we must remember that it was taken from everyone and on every market-day in the year. Then, secondly, stalls, booths, and even standing-room in the market-place were rented to the traders. A covered stall made of wood and canvas might cost as much as twelve pence to hire for the day, and an uncovered one eight pence, while a country woman, who brought in a basket of butter and another of cheese to sell, might pay two pence for room to stand or sit if she had sensibly carried her three-legged stool with her. Usually all the ordinary shops of the town were closed for the day and most of their owners would hire a market-stall themselves. The officials were kept very busy seeing that no one managed to sell anything without paying toll on it, which was what many tried to do. They had other duties too. Weights and measures had to be tested and a close watch kept for dishonest men who tried to trade unfairly. Before the market opened the quality and price of bread and ale were announced, and woe betide the man or woman found selling lightweight loaves or sour ale and wine. If they were caught they were usually tried on the spot in the special court where officials sat all day, ready to hear complaints and disputes and judge them by the market rules. The great thing was to show up dishonest traders publicly so that they would be avoided, and stocks and a pillory were usually to be found in every market-place where the guilty men had to sit or

The Shepherd The Fuller The Weaver

The Dyer The Merchant The Tailor

FROM SHEEP TO WEARER
(See pp. 154-6)

stand, being taunted and pelted with stale eggs or rotten onions. These market courts were often called pie-powder courts, which sounds a most senseless name until you begin to look into its meaning more closely. Then you discover that the words were a careless way of saying *pieds poudreux*, and if you translate that into English you will soon see why a pie-powder court was held at a market to which people came from long distances and often along very dusty roads.

After the market rules had been announced someone blew a trumpet or rang the church bell, and that was a sign that business might begin. Then the crowds of people, many from the town itself as well as the neighbourhood, began their chaffer and bargaining. Corn, bread, ale, rope, salt, nets, fish, butter, cheese, beans, and many other things changed hands, quarrels broke out and were settled one way or another, the nearby taverns and cook-shops did a roaring trade until the time came for the strangers to leave for home, and the stalls to be taken down, and the stocks emptied; and the market-place was left deserted except for prowling dogs on the look-out for scraps of food.

Far more important and exciting than the weekly markets were the fairs. These glorified markets could also only be held by 'licence and goodwill of the lord king', and every town did not have one. Fairs were held once a year, usually in the summer or autumn when the weather was likely to be fine, and were often connected with a saint's day or a pilgrimage. Some of them were very famous, not only all over the British Isles but in foreign countries too, and merchants from beyond the seas came to buy and sell at them. Among the best known were St. Giles's fair at Winchester; St. Bartholomew's in London; St. Botolph's at Boston, Lincolnshire; St. Ives in Huntingdon; and Stourbridge fair near Cambridge. St. Ives fair had been granted by King John to the abbot and monks of Ramsey Abbey in 1202, and it had 'to begin on the fourth day before the feast of St. Laurence and to endure for eight days'. The same sort of preparations went on as for markets, but on a much grander scale. Whole streets of stalls were put up, and the site was securely fenced round in the hope that no trader could get in without paying toll on his goods. Even so some would probably manage to squeeze through or under the fence unseen by the watchmen. There would be buyers and sellers of three different kinds bargaining at the fair. First, the local tradesmen and farmers; secondly, English merchants from other parts of the country; and thirdly, foreigners, men of Gascony selling wine, merchants from Flanders with fine cloth and from the Baltic ports with furs, wax, and steel, and most exciting of all

VISITING ST. IVES FAIR

perhaps, the merchants who brought goods from the East, spices, silk, almonds, raisins, ginger, pearls, and even monkeys.

There was something at the fair to please everyone. The nobleman who had come back from a crusade with new and expensive tastes could buy a gleaming sword in a richly worked scabbard from a dark-skinned merchant of Damascus or a keen hawk from a Lubeck man, and his lady could get fine silk and cloth for her dresses, as well as the best wax for her candles and ornaments for her hair. In fact in the middle of the thirteenth century the bishop of Lincoln strongly advised a noble lady to lay in stocks twice a year, going to Boston fair for her wine and wax and St. Ives for her dresses. There were spices which everyone had to have, for they helped to preserve food and also to hide the strong taste when it was not so very well preserved. Besides everyone loved spices, and not only the home-grown ones—housewives were glad to buy cinnamon, ginger, and pepper to add to garlic, onion, and parsley in their pottage.

Even for people who had little or nothing to spend the fair was still exciting. Not only did they see strange faces and foreign clothes, but there were all sorts of amusements for which they probably did not have to pay. Acrobats and tumblers would be up to the most extraordinary antics, clowns and jugglers kept the crowds in roars of laughter, and the men with performing animals, like the unhappy bear in the picture on page 139, were always a great attraction, especially when the bear got a little of his own back as he seems to be doing here. And people could always listen to the quack doctor promising wonderful cures for aches and pains, even if they could not afford his medicine, perhaps the very newest brand made of pounded beetles, which cured anything in three days. For a few pence a man could have a private consultation in the doctor's booth and explain his symptoms. Perhaps he had bad toothache, and the quack would tell him very seriously that: 'Wormes brede in the cheke teethe and this is known by their continuall digging and thirling. Take a candle of mutton fat and burn it as close as possible to the toothe, holding a basin of cold water beneath it. The worms which are gnawing the tooth will falle into the water to escape the heat of the candle.'

Watchmen were on duty every night while the fair lasted because of the two great dangers of fire and theft, but in spite of this, many a careful merchant preferred to spend the chilly nights on a wooden bed under the counter of his stall rather than run the risk of leaving his precious goods. The pie-powder court was kept very busy with cases, one moment perhaps dealing with an angry buyer who had bought twelve barrels of herrings and found that only three were good and the others were filled with sticklebacks and rotten fish, and the next with a hot-tempered fellow like Henry of Bythorp who, at St. Ives fair, set upon a rival, beat him and threw him into a well. Henry was fined six pence by the pie-powder court.

Fairs are not nearly so important as they used to be for buying and selling. There are now so many shops that you can buy what you want at any time without waiting for the eight days of St. Ives or the three weeks of Winchester fair. In fact we go to the fair chiefly for the amusements—the shies and round-abouts and rifle-ranges—and not for trade. But in the Middle Ages, when shops were few and sold only what the shopkeeper made himself, they were almost the only places where merchants could come from distant parts to sell their goods, and where people from far and wide could collect together to buy them. And they became more important as time went on because trade grew rapidly throughout the Middle Ages. In

England it became safer to travel, and that meant that more merchants could move about without fear of losing all their goods. The close link between this country and France after the Norman Conquest meant more coming and going across the Channel of people exchanging not only ideas but goods as well. And among the wide lands belonging to Henry II were parts of France famous for wine, and the Gascon wine merchant became a familiar figure in many parts of England. Then, of course, everyone who had been on a crusade had seen and bought new things on his travels and, when he came home, began to demand them over here. Sugar is a good example of something that was hardly known in England before the crusades, but afterwards it appeared here and there in small quantities, coming by way of Egypt and Persia, and slowly began to take the place of honey which for centuries had been the only sweetener until housewives could write to their husbands and say, 'I pray you to send me another sugar loaf for my old one is done'.

Of all trades the most important to England was the wool trade, and the wealth of this country was first built up from the fleeces of sturdy little black-faced sheep, and not from the coal and iron and steel which are so important now. If you ever visit the House of Lords you will see there facing the thrones for the king and queen a large object like a square sofa without arms. It is covered with fine red felted cloth, and is stuffed with wool from the British Isles and the countries of the Commonwealth. It is called the woolsack, on it sits the Lord Chancellor, one of the greatest officials of the realm, and it is there as a sign that once the wool trade was so important that much of the strength of England depended on it.

Many people earned a living from wool. There was the

TRANSPORT IN THE MIDDLE AGES
Horse-litter, country cart, and packhorse

farmer who kept the sheep, the fullers who cleaned it, the dyers, the weavers, the tailors, and above all the wool merchant. He was the man who went to the districts like the Cotswolds, Yorkshire, and Herefordshire where sheep flourished, bought the wool from the farmers and distributed it to the other workers. He had to get it sorted and packed into big bales and loaded on to the backs of sturdy pack-horses which carried it along the ancient roads, which had been used even before the Roman ones, to all parts of the country. Now much of the wool he bought was used in England but the greatest of all clothworkers in the world were the men of the Low Countries—Holland and Belgium as they are now—and these men depended largely on English wool for their work. So all through the Middle Ages the best of the crop was exported to them and it was a very profitable

business to be in. Many wool merchants made fortunes from it.
They began to have much money to spend, and so they built
larger houses for themselves, and bought finer furniture, tapestry
for the walls, and luxuries for their families. Some of them
spent part of their wealth on building beautiful churches to the
glory of God and in thankfulness for their prosperity, and these
churches still stand as you can see if you visit Northleach or
Fairford in Gloucestershire.

The king was always interested in this trade, for to tax wool
was a most convenient way of getting money. He ordered that
all wool for export must go to a certain town, called the staple
town, where his customs officers could inspect it and collect the
tax or duty on it. The staple town was not always the same, but
often it was Calais, which was an English possession for a long
time, and there all the merchants had to go to sell their wool and
all the foreign cloth traders had to come to buy it.

Because of all this wool merchants were most energetic
travellers, but they were not by any means the only ones. We
know that the king travelled far and wide throughout the land,
and so did many barons and knights, all moving from one of
their estates to another to collect and eat the produce of their
manors. But it is wrong to think that only the great ones of the
realm travelled, simply because we hear most about them. Even
today it is quite possible to meet people, especially in the
country, who have never seen the sea, or been to London, and
there would, of course, have been far more of them in the Middle
Ages. But a surprising number of quite ordinary unimportant
people did manage to make journeys of one kind or another.
They went, as we know to market and fairs, they went, as
William Merrygo went, on journeys for their lord as part of
their service to him. And they went on pilgrimages, which were

special journeys to holy places made for the honour of some saint and for the good of the pilgrim's soul. Crowds of people visited the tomb of Thomas à Becket or the shrine of Mary, the mother of Christ, at Walsingham in Norfolk, and many, braving the perils of the sea and unknown countries, went to the home of St. James at Compostella in Spain, to Rome, or to the Holy Land itself. Carrying pilgrims across the seas was an important trade in some places. Bristol merchants had ships especially set apart to take the travellers who were going to visit Compostella. In 1456 a merchant called Thomas Sturny of Bristol was licensed to carry sixty pilgrims in his ship, the *Katherine Sturny*. It was always safer, and much more amusing, for pilgrims to travel in companies, and when Geoffrey Chaucer, the poet who lived for a time at the court of Edward III, went on a pilgrimage to Canterbury he described the people he went with. Some of them were of gentle birth—there was a knight who had already been to Palestine, his son, a gay young squire richly dressed and mounted on a fine horse, and the prioress of a convent, who was very refined and had beautiful table manners. But there were other much humbler people too, in the same company of twenty-nine pilgrims—a miller, a ploughman, a sailor, a reeve, an innkeeper, a goodwife, and a parish priest.

All Chaucer's pilgrims travelled from London to Canterbury on horseback, but there must have been many more who went on foot through England, and with them the pedlars, minstrels, quack doctors, and others who were going from fair to fair, or to outlying villages and manor houses. Many of them would sleep among the straw or rushes on the floor of some castle hall or tavern. They might stop at a monastery and get food and beds free of any charge, for it was the duty of the monks to give food and shelter to strangers. But wherever they went they loved to pass the time by telling stories and singing songs, hoping that wherever they spent the night they would find good ale, and warmth, and a host who said, 'Please God—you shall be well and comfortably lodged here, save that there is a great peck of rats and mice.'

CANTERBURY PILGRIMS

Pilgrimages, particularly the pilgrimage to the shrine of St. Thomas at Canterbury were the popular holidays of that time

Henry III and Simon de Montfort

KING JOHN was forced to agree to the reforms demanded in Magna Carta, and this long document contained some clauses which were to be highly important later on. But the mere sealing of it was not enough to make certain that England was well governed from 1215 onward. John was followed by his son, Henry III, a much more pleasant person than his father but almost as unsatisfactory as a king, and his reign was full of trouble and strife. He was only nine years old when he became king in 1216, and for the next sixteen years the country was well governed by Hubert de Burgh, the Regent of England, helped at first by William Marshall, Earl of Pembroke. But Pembroke died after two years, and in 1232 Henry III dismissed Hubert and began to rule for himself helped by a set of advisers who, although they were often quite able men, were very much disliked by many of the most important people in the country, and in their eyes could do nothing right.

Henry's court was crowded with the French-Italian relations of his wife, Eleanor of Provence, and Henry seemed to prefer these newly arrived foreigners to Englishmen. He certainly showered titles and lands and money on them, which was much resented by the English barons, who found themselves shut out from all the most important positions about the king. Another grievance was the king's attitude to the Pope (Alexander IV). Like Edward the Confessor, Henry was a most pious man, and he usually neither wished nor dared to oppose the Pope in anything. He allowed Alexander to raise enormous sums of money in England to pay for his own wars, and also to appoint three hundred foreign clergy to English churches. Few of these men ever came to live and work over here, but they took the incomes from the parishes, and though substitutes were appointed to the work of these absentee clergy, the fact that they were appointed at all was most unpopular with people of all classes, barons, clergy, and commons. At last the barons and clergy decided to oppose the king's bad government, as they had his father's, and to demand reforms. The clergy were headed by Robert Grosseteste, bishop of Lincoln, and the barons by Simon de Montfort. Simon had married the king's sister, but he had quarrelled with Henry and joined the restive barons.

The king's enemies met at Oxford in 1258, where they drew up a set of demands and plans called the Provisions of Oxford. Henry was forced by threat of war to agree to them, although it meant practically handing over his power to a council of fifteen barons led by Simon. But soon he obtained permission from the Pope to break his promise, and then raised an army to punish the barons. He was defeated at the battle of Lewes in 1264, and made prisoner, and Simon de Montfort became for a time the real master of England.

But not for long. He could not control the barons, who soon became jealous of him and annoyed by his high-handed ways. Simon struggled hard to keep his hold on the country, and in his efforts he tried an experiment which was afterwards very important. In 1265 he called a King's Council to try and get more support. Now the Council had often been held before by kings of England who called to it their chief tenants, just as any lord of a manor called his to the manor court. The king's tenants were the great men of the realm, earls, barons, bishops, and abbots. Simon guessed that many of these great men would not help him, and he only called twenty-three to the council. But in order to strengthen his position he invited as well the counties to send two knights, and the towns which were friendly to him to send two burgesses. This was a good idea and was used again after Simon was dead, but it did not help him much at the time. The very same year Henry's eldest son Prince Edward rallied the royal forces again and this time defeated Simon at the Battle of Evesham (1265) where the earl was killed. The prince took over the government from his feeble father, promising to rule according to Magna Carta, and in his very capable hands the country lay quiet for the remaining seven years of Henry III's life, and during his own long reign.

12. Edward I. Wales and Scotland

EDWARD I, who became king in 1272, was another remarkable Plantagenet. To look at he must have been almost as impressive as Richard Cœur de Lion, for he, too, was so tall that he stood head and shoulders above other people and was 'as straight as a palm', which probably means as straight as one of the long shoots of a willow tree, not the wavy date-palm. His hair changed colour twice during his lifetime; it was very fair when he was a boy, black when he grew up, and silver in later life 'so that he seemed as white as a swan'. His left eyelid drooped curiously. Even when he grew old he rode as nimbly as a boy, and he took so much exercise that he never became fat, and was hardly ever ill. Besides this he had a good brain and was cool in danger. Like his great grandfather Henry II he was very observant and missed little that went on, and he was clever enough to learn by other peoples' mistakes and so avoid much

HEADPIECE. The Hue and Cry in action. If the man could reach the church, he could claim sanctuary (safety) in it trouble. When he became king he already knew a good deal about the work of ruling men, for he had controlled lands of his own in England and France, he had travelled to Italy, and been to Palestine on a crusade. He had seen his own father, Henry III, make almost as many mistakes as his grandfather John, for Henry had reigned for fifty-six years and been in continual difficulties for much of that time. Henry III was not a bad man like John, but he was weak and yet headstrong and wilful, and not by nature fitted to be a king. One of the best things he did was to rebuild in the beautiful Early English style the great church of Edward the Confessor at Westminster, and all his life he loved colour, and jewels, and metalwork. But his mistakes in government were many, and civil war broke out during his reign between the king and a party of barons led by Simon de Montfort. These men drew up a list of demands to which Henry was obliged to submit, and for a short time Simon was the real ruler of England.

But Edward I was a very different person from Henry III. He was hard working and efficient, and he constantly visited many parts of his kingdom to see that his officials were, too. He was also anxious to govern, as far as he could, with all classes of people co-operating and agreeing—not only the barons and the clergy, but the burgesses of towns and the country knights as well. Very soon after his coronation, which was a most gorgeous affair with feasts lasting for fifteen days, he sent out officials everywhere to inquire into the general state of the land, much in the same way that William the Conqueror did. When he heard of things that were wrong Edward made laws to improve them. One, passed in 1278, called the Statute of Gloucester, inquired by what right, *quo warranto*, certain men held their own courts on their estates and kept out the king's judges, and

another, the Statute of Winchester, in 1285 set out to make the
roads safer for travellers by ordering brushwood and bushes to
be cut down for two hundred feet on each side of the public
highway. It also declared that town gates must be closed at
night and that every man must be prepared to pursue robbers
and evil-doers. This pursuit was known as the 'Hue and Cry';
every able-bodied person ran at top speed after the criminal,
and yelled as loudly as possible so that all might hear and join
in the chase.

Now when Edward drew up such laws as these he usually
did so in the presence of his Great Council, which consisted
of the most important barons, bishops, and abbots of the
realm. Sometimes, however, he wanted to be sure that the
other classes of Englishmen, which we mentioned just now,
would agree with what he was doing and so make things work
more smoothly and efficiently. For instance, in 1275 when the
king needed money, he called a meeting much bigger than the
Great Council at Westminster, which agreed to the 'great and
ancient custom' and gave him and his heirs the right to put a tax
of seven shillings and sixpence per sack on the export of wool
and leather. Twenty years later, in 1295, he called a still bigger
meeting. There were many dangers threatening the country at
the time, and Edward again needed money for defence. He
summoned to Westminster the great barons, the bishops, the
important abbots, but also two knights from every county and
two burgesses from every town which held a royal charter. And
at the bottom of a summons sent out to call them together
some clerk wrote, 'What touches all should have the consent of
all'. This collection, in 1295, of the men of the realm was very
important because it became a pattern for future meetings, and
so it is sometimes called the Model Parliament. No one quite

knows when that word 'parliament' was first used to describe this assembly, but it is perfectly clear why it was used, because the king and his subjects were discussing, talking over certain matters, and the word comes from 'parlement' the French word for talking. It was obviously a wise and sensible thing for Edward I to call his parliaments for advice and help, and besides he could explain his own point of view to them personally, but he had no idea that one day all the business of governing and making laws would be in their hands.

You might expect that a powerful king like Edward I would try to regain the lands in France which John Lackland had lost, but he did not do this. Instead, he set himself to master the outlying parts of the British Isles, Wales, and Scotland.

Wales was known to its own people as 'Cymru' or the land of comrades, and as we saw in Chapter 1[1] it was the part of the country west of the Severn and the Dee to which the Britons had fled when the Anglo-Saxons conquered England. They never became a united people, for they were divided into tribes and spent much time and energy fighting one another. They particularly enjoyed this occupation, partly because they thought it wrong to die in their beds and noble to fall in battle, but also because, as very few of them were settled in villages or towns but lived in rough huts made of lopped trees and wattle, they did not mind leaving these quite cheerfully when an enemy drew near. They simply packed their goods on to the backs of sturdy little horses, drove their cattle before them, and disappeared into the mountains from which they carried out fierce raids and attacks on the foe. They had never mixed much with their neighbours in England. One Anglo-Saxon king, Offa by name, had built a great dyke from the Dee to the Wye as a boundary between

[1] See p. 14.

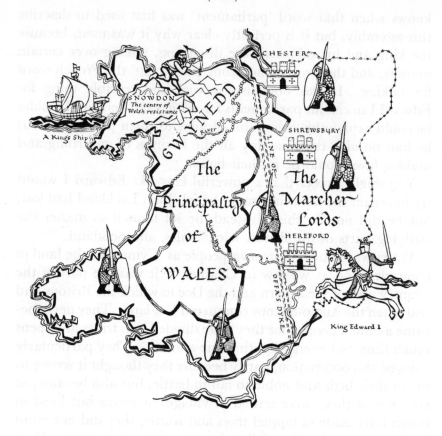

WALES IN 1277

In that year Edward I surrounded Llewellyn's eyrie in the Snowdon mountains and
starved him into surrender. During the next ten years the royal castles of Conway,
Carnarvon, Beaumaris, and Harlech were built

Welsh and English lands, and except for annoying raids across this boundary the Welsh kept very much to themselves.

When William the Conqueror came things changed a good deal. William set up three great estates on the Welsh Marches (or border) and gave them to the earls of Chester, Shrewsbury, and Hereford. They were to be the watch-dogs of the Marches. But these Marcher lords and others with smaller estates in those parts were not content to be merely that, and they were so far away and so hard to reach that, though they did homage for their lands to the king, they were really quite independent and behaved very much as they liked. Gradually they pressed with their armed bands farther and farther into Wales, until they had devoured large bites of the centre and the south. They settled themselves chiefly in the valleys, which are still studded with the ruins of their grim castles, and the Welsh chieftains took to the hill-tops. Only the very mountainous north-west part of the land, called Gwynedd, was left completely in the hands of a prince of Wales, and when Edward I became king of England the ruling prince was called Llewellyn. Now Llewellyn was not content with his share of Wales and he had gradually reconquered much of the centre of the land, and perhaps dreamed of driving out the English altogether. He proudly refused to attend Edward's coronation and do homage to him as his overlord. In 1276 by a stroke of luck Edward captured the Lady Eleanor de Montfort, who was engaged to Llewellyn, as she was on her way to Wales for her marriage, and he held her as a hostage and went himself with his army to bring the prince to terms. Llewellyn disappeared quickly into the mountains round Snowdon, believing that he could hold out indefinitely there. But no one can hope to do that for long without good supplies of food, and most of his supplies came from the fertile island of Anglesey.

Edward soon cut off all Llewellyn's corn by blockading Anglesey
with his fleet, and before long the prince was starved into surrender. Then Edward allowed him to marry Eleanor, and, in
fact, went to the wedding himself, but he took from Llewellyn
all his conquered lands, leaving him only Gwynedd, and for
that the prince had to do homage to the king of England as his
overlord.

Llewellyn was unhappy and angry about this arrangement;
he hated the restrictions on his power, and felt that Edward
listened to the tales of his enemies, and did not treat him fairly.
Five years later, in 1287, he and his brother David rebelled, and
Edward decided that Gwynedd must finally be conquered and
Llewellyn deposed. Again the English ships and soldiers block-
aded the wild land about Snowdon where the Welsh had their
headquarters, and this time Llewellyn broke free and escaped
through Edward's lines. But soon afterwards he was killed in
battle, and six months later David, too, was caught and killed.
Gwynedd passed completely into Edward's hands and into
those of the Marcher lords who had helped him a good deal
during the campaign. Would he be able to hold it and pacify
the Welsh?

He was nothing if not thorough, and he set about the problem
as efficiently as he did everything else. Splendid new castles
were built at Conway, Caernarvon, Criccieth, and Harlech, and
filled with English soldiers; new towns grew up round them and
English burgesses were encouraged to live in them. Thus Wales
became part of Edward's kingdom, but the Welsh themselves
were not forced to become Englishmen, for they kept their own
language and many of their laws and customs. But there was
still one thing which made the king uneasy. Just six months
before Llewellyn was killed his wife bore him a little daughter

CHANCELLOR AND CHIEF JUSTICES ON THE WOOLSACK

christened Gwenllian. She was the last of the royal family of
Wales and, baby as she was, Edward was afraid that when she
grew up the Welsh might rally round her and rebel once more.
So he took her away from Wales and had her sent right to the
far-eastern side of England, to the convent at Sempringham in
Lincolnshire, where she was put in charge of the nuns. There
she lived all her life in the flat fenlands far away from the
mountains of her native land, and there she died in 1337 at the
age of fifty-five, quite forgotten by the Welsh.

Edward I had made himself the lord of Wales, but he could
not do the same in Scotland, though he tried very hard. Oddly
enough, another small girl comes into this story, too. In 1286,
four years after the convent doors of Sempringham had shut on
Gwenllian, the princess ot Wales, Alexander III, king of Scotland, fell from his horse as he rode along the edge of the sea and

was killed. He left no son, and the heir to his throne was his little granddaughter, Margaret, the Maid of Norway. Now no woman had ever reigned over the turbulent kingdom of Scotland, and when Edward I proposed that the Maid should marry his own son and heir, Edward of Caernarvon, and that they should rule jointly, the Scottish barons agreed, and the Maid left Norway to come to Scotland. This was a clever move on Edward's part, for it meant that after his death the two countries would be united under his son. But the rough sea-crossing was too much for Margaret, she was only sixteen, and perhaps not very strong, and when she reached the Orkney Islands she fell ill and died, and with her passed the peace of Scotland for many years.

Thirteen distant relatives of Alexander III immediately claimed the throne, and the question was, who should decide between them? Edward offered his help, knowing very well that he could get something out of it, and with the aid of a hundred and four advisers, some Scots, some Englishmen, he chose John Balliol, on condition that the new king did homage to him as overlord. None of the Scots took this homage very seriously, but Edward did, and he soon began to behave as if he were their master, issuing orders, and treating the new King John in a most humiliating way. At last, by 1295, the Scottish people got tired of this and they made it plain to their barons and to John himself that their king must refuse to behave any longer as a mere English subject. But as soon as he did refuse Edward collected an army and set off to punish him. In the wars that followed the Scottish barons were at first little help to their country. Most of them had estates in England as well as Scotland, and some, like John Balliol, whose name was originally Bailleul, in France as well. They were afraid of offending

MOUNTED SCOTTISH RAIDERS
Early fourteenth century

Edward I and losing their English lands, and yet at the same time afraid of offending the Scottish people by doing everything he wanted. Because of these things many of the Scottish barons changed sides as often as a dozen times.

To many of the English soldiers Scotland must have seemed a wild and terrifying place as they marched through what one man called 'Mountains, valleys, rocks, and many evil passages and marvellous great marshes'. They were amazed by the speed at which the Scots travelled on their little horses, and still more by the strange food they ate. Each of them carried a broad plate of metal on his saddle and a little sack of oatmeal. When they stopped for a meal they lit a fire and laid the metal plate over it. Then they mixed some oatmeal into a thin paste with water, and cast the paste on to the hot metal and produced a thin brittle little cake—in fact, an oatcake. They would live for weeks on this food, with a drink of river water, unless they managed to kill a cow or a sheep, when they would cook it in its skin and eat the half-sodden flesh with immense relish. But with all their toughness and bravery the Scots were ill armed compared with the English, and Edward's army quickly overcame them, especially when John Balliol was captured and they were without a leader. Having removed John from his throne Edward returned home, leaving some of his officials to keep order. He actually carried with him to England the sacred stone on which all kings of Scotland sat at their coronation, and he meant by this to show the Scots that they would never have another king of their own. But he was wrong. Hardly was his back turned than they rose in rebellion led by William Wallace, a simple knight of Elderslie in Renfrewshire. He was so humble a man that the great barons despised him and gave him no help, but under him the common people of Scotland fought like tigers for their liberty. Unlike the richer barons Wallace and his followers had no lands in England or France. All they owned was on the soil of Scotland, and they had no difficulty in making up their minds which side to fight on. They hated the English sheriffs that Edward had left behind to rule them and tax them for a foreign king, and even more, perhaps, they hated their own nobles who had allowed that foreign king to take control. Wallace and his men were at first successful; they won the battle of Stirling in 1297 and drove the English commander from the land, but next year Edward himself reappeared with an army at his back. And his men bore with them weapons which were deadly to the Scots. These were the long-bows which later were to make English archers famous everywhere, and, oddly enough, they were first used by the Welsh who had so recently been defeated. In fact, Edward took many Welsh archers to Scotland with him, men who only a short time before had been his enemies. The long-bows were five feet long and the men who used them had to be able to draw the cord back past the right ear, instead of only to the chest as with a short bow. With its great size and this added pull the long-bow shot an arrow which could pierce an oak door four inches thick, and go clean through a strong iron breastplate. With his archers first pouring arrows among them from two hundred yards away and his cavalry following with a charge, Edward mangled the Scots at the battle of Falkirk in 1298. For a time the resistance movement was broken and Wallace fled, an outlaw, into hiding. The Scots had fought bravely and they had been helped by the French who were at war with Edward at this time and were always willing to make matters as difficult for him as they could.

For seven years after Falkirk Edward ruled Scotland through a council, and no doubt he hoped that trouble was at an end. But again he was wrong. There was living at his court a Scottish nobleman named Robert Bruce, grandson of one of the thirteen who had put in a claim when Alexander III died. One dark winter night in 1305 Bruce fled from England and had himself crowned king of Scotland. He was not a particularly promising leader. To begin with, he had already given in to Edward several times in order to save the estates he had in England. Then he lost his first battle, and for years after could only wander, homeless and outlawed, in the highlands. It seemed unlikely that the crown would ever sit firmly on Bruce's head, for he had many enemies. But in 1307 King Edward, coming north again to subdue the restless Scots, fell ill and died, and his son, Edward of Caernarvon, who liked swimming and rowing so much better than fighting, returned home. Robert Bruce struggled on against his Scottish enemies for seven years longer and slowly broke their power. Then at last, in 1314, Edward II pulled himself together and raised an army to invade Scotland. Not far from Stirling, on Midsummer Day 1314, the two armies met beside a small stream called the Bannock Burn. Bruce and his men were fighting for their liberty and well they knew it.

> Now's the day and now's the hour,
> See the front o' battle lour!
> See approach proud Edward's power,
> Chains and slaverie.

But the chains were never fastened. Battered by furious attacks from the Scots Edward's army fell into mad confusion and he soon lost all control, and fled from the Bannock Burn leaving thousands of his men to die, and the Scots to rejoice in their freedom.

Edward I's great plan for uniting England, Wales, and Scotland had failed. The Scots had kept their independence and their king was free from English overlords. But still there was no peace between the countries. Year after year the Scots rode across the border and raided the north of England. They carried off cattle, corn, and provisions, and they burned castles and farms and churches. In spite of the fact that in 1328 Edward III made the Peace of Northampton with Robert Bruce and acknowledged him to be the rightful king of Scotland, the habit of border warfare was strong both with Englishmen and Scots, so strong that they did not lose it until long after 1603, when James VI of Scotland became James I of England too. Then, more than 300 years after Edward I had tried to unite the two countries by force, they became one kingdom quite peacefully. But until that time the Scots were always ready to make trouble for the king of England whenever he was in difficulties elsewhere, and in doing so they could nearly always count on help from another enemy of England—the king of France.

ENGLISH LONG-BOW MAN ABOUT 1300

The skill of the English foot soldiers
with the long-bow ended the power
of knights on horseback

EDWARD I was a strong and able Plantagenet, sandwiched between two far less successful ones, his father Henry III, and his son Edward II. He was clever enough to use Simon de Montfort's idea of summoning two knights from the shires and two burgesses from certain towns to Parliament to strengthen his own power; he passed many wise and useful laws, and he made himself popular and respected by being a keen and often successful fighter. He conquered Wales, and nearly conquered Scotland. But in 1307 he died while on his way north to subdue Robert the Bruce. Edward II—known as Edward of Caernarvon—could not live up to the standard set by his father. Although one of the most magnificent of the Plantagenet family to look at, tall, powerful, and athletic, he often behaved in a thoughtless, undignified way, and disliked concentrating for long at a time on the business of ruling England. He took no interest in fighting or in knightly contests, and much preferred swimming, or cutting the hedges of his royal estates, which shocked his subjects, especially the nobles to whom fighting was the most important matter in life. Edward's defeat at Bannock Burn in 1314 rankled badly with them, and so did the favours he showered on his frivolous friend, Piers Gaveston. He was soon in conflict with the barons over the government of England, and in 1326 his wife, Isabella, deserted him, and led a large number of them against him. Edward had to flee for his life, and tried to reach Lundy Island off the coast of Devon, but he was caught and made to resign the crown to his son, then thirteen years old. Queen Isabella and her friends ruled in the name of the young Edward III, while the wretched Edward II was shut up in Berkeley Castle, Gloucestershire, and in 1327 murdered there.

13. Education

WHEN the word education is mentioned today nine people out of every ten think first of all of books, pencils, pens, ink, and going to school, and these nine would consider that in the Middle Ages very few children had any education at all. And in a way they would be quite right, for only a small number of boys and even fewer girls learned to read and write and to feel at home with books. There were three different places in which they could get this kind of learning. Sometimes the parish priest would teach one or two boys their alphabet and a little penmanship, enough for them to read the services and possibly rise to some minor post in the Church, such as doorkeeper and sexton. If any of these boys happened to be the sons of villeins

HEADPIECE. William of Wykeham with Winchester and New College banner. William of Wykeham was not only bishop of Winchester but also one of the king's councillors. He was interested in education and founded Winchester College and New College, Oxford

they could not, as we know, have even this minute quantity of teaching without permission from the lord, for the very fact of their wanting it might mean that they were dreaming of some other occupation than working all their life on the land, and that the lord was therefore in danger of losing their services.

Secondly, there were the monastery schools. These were not open to any boy who wanted to go to them, and it is quite wrong to think they were. They were meant only for those who were going to become monks, and though, no doubt, a few others slipped in here and there, the abbots and priors were always trying to insist on this rule. Because they were preparing boys to enter the monastery the education which the monks gave was almost entirely concerned with religion, with the rule of the community and its services, though of course this meant as well some reading, writing, and Latin.

Thirdly, there were the grammar schools, most of which were attached to large churches and cathedrals, though as time went on others were founded which were free of such ties. For instance, in 1382 William of Wykeham started his famous school at Winchester, which took seventy boys and was the largest in England; and sixty years after, in 1440, Henry VI set up the grammar school of Eton. The title of public school was given for the first time to Eton, and it meant simply that boys might come there from anywhere in the country and not only from the Windsor neighbourhood.

The grammar schools concentrated with might and main on the teaching of Latin grammar, for, as Latin was the universal language of learning and religion everywhere in Europe, all their pupils had to be able to read, write, and speak it correctly. And it was a most useful thing, for it meant that an educated person could get on very well in any foreign country even though he could not speak its language. But Latin, with some mathematics, was about all a grammar-school boy did learn, and to many of them the lessons must have been deadly dull. If a boy was clever enough to go farther he passed on to a university, that is, a centre where the more difficult, but certainly more interesting, branches of learning were taught. In England after the thirteenth century he would have gone to Oxford or Cambridge, but he might prefer to attend one of the older universities on the Continent, such as Paris, Bologna in Italy, and Salerno in Italy, too, and very famous for the study of medicine. Often he took a long time over his studies and visited several foreign universities as well as the English ones. When he reached the schools at such places, he plunged into logic, astronomy, music, and more mathematics, and Latin, even though he might be only fourteen or fifteen years old—for boys went to the universities at a much earlier age than they do now, which perhaps accounts for the fact that Oxford scholars were solemnly warned that they must not play marbles!

The hours in a medieval school were appallingly long. Lessons began at 6 o'clock in the morning and went on solidly till eleven, with a break of fifteen minutes at 9 o'clock, just as you are arriving at school, for breakfast and prayers. Dinner came at 11, a sample meal being 'peassoupe, bredde, and ale'; and then mercifully there was a long break before afternoon school which began at 1 o'clock and went on till 5 p.m. You had one free afternoon in the week and that was on Sunday, but there were always the Church festivals and saints' days, which meant a holy-day (holiday) when no work was done. There were no organized games in these schools. The boys amused themselves with running, jumping, wrestling, throwing, and playing football round about the houses and streets, as madly as the apprentices did in their spare time, and just as dangerously. And they could always roam in the woods and fields, and go swimming and fishing in the streams in summer, and slide on the frozen ponds in winter, all of which was good fun. The worst part of the grammar schools must certainly have been that the lessons were so long and often so dull, and that boys were urged on to work much more by a bundle of springy twigs than by common sense or kindness. In fact one well-beaten schoolboy wrote a poem about his troubles and what he wished could happen to the master. In it he says that learning is strange work and that he hates Monday morning and that:

> The birchen twiggis be so sharpe
> It maketh me have a faint heart
> I would my master were an hare
> And all his bookes hounds were
> And I myself a jolly hunter
> To blow my horn I would not spare
> For if he were dead I would not care.

Parents were just as severe as schoolmasters with their children, and in one book, which explains how to bring up a family properly, they were given this piece of advice: 'If your children are cheeky, take a smart rod and beat them in a row.' One hard-hearted mother Mistress Anne Paston, wrote to say that she hoped the schoolmaster would 'truly belash' her son Clement, and she would give him ten marks for the labour, and she was not at all an unusually cruel person. No wonder that children were then far more afraid of their parents than they ever are now, and when they wrote to them began, 'Right reverend and worshipful father', instead of simply 'Dear Dad'.

But though so few people went to school and had any book learning when they were young, practically everyone had some

The birchen twiggis be so sharpe
It maketh me have a faint heart

sort of training for the work they were going to do or the life they were going to lead, even if they only picked it up as they went along.

For instance in the village the child of a freeman or villein began when very small to learn about the country skills and crafts that his father and mother knew. Boys and girls alike went into the fields with the grown-up people and did what jobs they could, scaring birds, picking stones, helping with hay-making and harvest, and gradually absorbing the 'obstinate old way' of husbandry, that is, of growing crops and rearing animals. The father who was a clever thatcher, hedger, smith, or carpenter passed on his knowledge to his son, and every mother taught, or tried to teach, her daughter all the domestic science she knew. Girls, in fact, had a sort of double training, for they were often as skilled at farming as the boys, but also had to be able to cook, spin, weave, and preserve food by salting and drying, as well as cure sickness with herb medicines, and do a hundred other things. In fact it did not matter much whether a girl lived in a cottage or a castle; she had, if she was to run her home well, to know far more about every side of housecraft than most women do now, for she had few shops and no laundries, no clinics or hospitals to turn to.

The children of the manor house or the castle led a very different life from their father's tenants or the children of ordinary townspeople. Both boys and girls were usually sent away from home when they were quite small—seven years old perhaps—to be brought up in some other household, in a distant manor house or a nobleman's castle, or perhaps even in the royal court itself. Occasionally the girls went to board in convents, though, if they did, like the boys in monastery schools, they were supposed to be trained as nuns. Wherever a girl was

YOUNG LADIES DANCING

sent, however, her training was about the same. She learned to run a household, unless she was exceedingly well born and noble, and even then she had to know how to manage her servants, to sew and embroider, to sing and dance. She might possibly learn to read, and even to write, but this was uncommon and very much by the way. She would be taught to ride, for, if she was lucky, she might sometimes hunt with the boys and men. But for many well-born girls life must have been at times terribly dull and boring, far more so than for the hard-working daughter of a villager or a townsman. Fighting was the chief occupation of a gentleman, and from this she was barred. When she grew up there were only two things she could do. Either she could marry or she could go into a convent, and many a girl became a nun because she was not wanted in her home, had not married, and there was simply nothing else for her to do.

Her brother on the other hand had a far more exciting and interesting time. When he went away from home he became a page to some suitable lord, and was carefully trained for his future career, which was to become a knight. This meant that he must learn good manners and skill in fighting and hunting. It was not particularly important for him to learn to read, but as there are some ancient books of etiquette and instructions written specially for these boys of good birth, some of them must have been able to read. One of these, called the *Babees Book*, tells us exactly how a page ought to behave at almost every hour of the day. He is told to get up early, wash his face and hands (being careful to see that his nails are clean), and comb his hair. He is to say his prayers or, better still, go to church and hear Mass. He must be careful to say 'Good morning' to everyone he meets, and not start the day by looking lumpish. Table manners are most important, and the page is told over and over again to look after other people at meals and not grab the best food, never to fill his mouth full 'as a pigge', nor to speak with it full. He must not pick his teeth with his knife, a clean stick is the best thing to use. His general manner must be good, too. He should stand up straight, not lounge against a post, and he should on no account scratch himself or sniff in public. A page had to wait upon his lord and lady with great care, bowing when he spoke to them, and never wearing a cap in their presence. He had always to offer wine to his lord on bended knee, and bring water for him to wash his hands in after every meal.

All the time the page was being taught graceful manners he was learning many other things as well. He had of course to be an excellent horseman, and to understand the use of weapons and the correct wearing of armour. At first he was not nearly strong enough to bear the weight of full armour and he had to

A PAGE'S FIRST LESSON IN EQUITATION

A page learnt to ride when very young. Little by little he had to get used to managing his armour as well as his horse. This page is wearing helmet and foot-coverings, and is carrying his shield. The weight obviously affects his balance

get accustomed to it by degrees, besides learning the correct way of putting it on and getting out of it again, which the unfortunate boy in the picture above does not seem to have grasped at all well. The laws of jousting at tournaments had to be learned as well as the elaborate rules for hunting and hawking. Hawks had to have a very careful training for the chase, which began after they had lost their baby down and grown their first proper plumage, and a gentleman had to know all about it. Usually the birds were all kept in a special building near the stables called the mews, which was given this name because of the peculiar cat-like cry or mew that the hawks make, but

often people kept their favourites with them indoors. A trained
hawk wore a little hood of very soft leather until just before
he was released to search for prey, otherwise be became excited
and quite unmanageable when he saw what was going on
around. He stood perched on his master's wrist, his sharp
claws prevented from digging into it by a thickly-padded
gauntlet glove. On one of his legs he had a little ring to
which a thin leather strap like a dog-leash was fastened, and he
could not fly till this was undone. He also had a tiny bell
attached either to a leg or to a strong feather in his tail so that
he could be traced in long grass and bushes by its sound. A
page had to learn how to handle his hawk properly, so that
when out hunting he could slip the leash and hood off neatly,
and throw the bird up into the air from his wrist.[1] It would
hover overhead until it saw a rabbit, or hare, or partridge on
the ground below and then plunge down on it with such force
that the poor beast was killed almost at once. The next thing
was to stop the hawk from devouring the prey, for it always had
to be taken out to the chase hungry or it would not hunt. This
was done rather cleverly by waving a lure over its head. The
lure was simply a brightly coloured tassel, but while the hawk
was in training a small piece of meat was always fastened under-
neath, which showed as the tassel was waved over its head. The
hawk always remembered the coloured lure and connected it
with food, and so it would move towards it and leave the newly-
caught prey for the huntsman to pick up.

When a page reached the age of fourteen he became a squire.
By this time he was expected to be courteous, and brave, able to
sing, and recite poems, to play the harp or pipe, and help to
amuse company in every way. He had to know how to carve

[1] See the illustration on p. 188.

meat at table, hand the wine, and his own table manners had to be excellent. He might become a squire of the bedchamber in which case he looked after his lord's clothes, brushing them at least once a week for fear of moths. At night he would help his master to bed, taking off his robe, shoes, socks, and breeches, combing his hair, and handing him a night-cap if he wanted one. Finally he would set a night-light beside him, drive out the cat and dog, and with a low bow retire himself.

This knightly education was a hard training and went on for years—page, squire, and finally knight were the stages—and the story of the final stage is told in another chapter.

But perhaps the soundest education of all was that which, in the Middle Ages, was given to an apprentice by his master. It was thorough, and it was useful, just as useful as learning to fight correctly. It was as satisfying as farming, but it carried with it freedom which was denied to many boys who grew up in the country ways. Take for example Simon Winterflood's young son, Matthew, who hated his father's trade of fishmongering and who longed to be a mason. His father bound him as an apprentice to a friend of his, a well-known craftsman of the mason's guild, named Master John Malet. The two men signed the agreement which said that for seven years, that is till he was fourteen, Matthew was to live with Master Malet and be taught all the secrets and mystery of the mason's craft. Matthew himself promised to obey his master, to work hard, and not to run away. Some apprentices who had bad masters did run away and broke their word but Matthew never wanted to. He was fascinated by the colour and feel of the different kinds of stone they worked in, and the shapes into which it could be wrought, and his head was always full of new patterns which he wanted to carve. Master Malet honestly taught him all he knew and helped him to learn to read and write as well, and when the seven years were over Matthew was well on the way towards being a highly skilled craftsman, taking an immense pride in every piece of work he did, trained to do one thing very well and completely satisfied in doing it.

RELEASING A HAWK
This was done by letting it free
(unleashing it) and at the same
time unhooding it

14. The Court

In the Middle Ages the king of England was a wanderer. The royal lands in France often took him abroad, even if he did not go on a crusade as Richard Cœur de Lion and Edward I did, and in England, too, he was constantly on the move. He usually led the army in person when it went to war, and he travelled a great deal on government business. But even more he moved because, like all great men, he had to live chiefly on the produce of his many manors. It was easier on the whole for him to go to the manor than for its produce to be sent to him, and although no king could possibly visit all the royal estates each year—for there were between fourteen and fifteen hundred of them—he went to as many as possible. Edward I, for instance, stayed in seventy-five different places in one year, or about three each

HEADPIECE. Man-at-arms, jester, and page

fortnight, and his son, Edward of Caernarvon, was also perpetually wandering from the time he was eight years old. Only during the winter when weather was bad and roads difficult was the young prince able to settle down for a few months at his house at King's Langley in Hertfordshire. He would have liked to spend much more time there than he did, for he loved the place. He had a fine hall with two fire-places and walls brightly painted with red and yellow shields and a picture of knights riding to a tournament. He had stables, too, where in 1292, besides his horses which he dearly loved, lived a camel and a lion cub; and there was a river with two little islands in it where he liked to swim. But if Edward of Caernarvon longed to stay at King's Langley because he was far more interested in country life, and rowing, and swimming, than in anything else, he was probably an exception, for most kings and their sons took their restless life as a matter of course.

With the king went his household—the court—and a very large one it was consisting of his high officers of state and their assistants, servants of every kind, and of course his family and personal friends. In fact wherever the king went a large train of people and belongings went too, and the organization was very hard work. The household was divided into several departments. One of them, under the steward, arranged for food and drink, and huge quantities were needed, for not only must the king himself be fed, but the wages of the servants down to the smallest scullion consisted partly of so much food and drink each day. The steward sent his scouts, called purveyors, far ahead of the royal party to make sure that there would be enough provisions. They were most unpopular people, for they could commandeer anything they wanted, and were not always very prompt in paying for it. Besides they often helped them-

THE KING'S BEDROOM
The boy in the picture is a royal page

selves to a good deal as well. When William Rufus was king their behaviour was abominable, and if it was known that the king was coming into the district the people fled to the woods and hid, taking as many of their belongings as they could carry.

Another department was reponsible for the king's bedchamber and wardrobe. Its head was the chamberlain, and he was responsible for all the furniture, bedding, lighting, and heating of the private rooms of the royal family. For instance he saw to it that everything in the king's chamber was ready for him when he arrived, that the rushes on the floor were fresh and plentiful, and that the keeper of the hearth had a fire burning when the weather was cold. There were squires of the bedchamber in this department to help the king remove his armour and change his clothes, and a water-bearer who was paid three pence every time he prepared the royal bath-tub. The chamberlain's assistants looked after the king's clothes and armour, and hard work they must have had with the cleaning of the armour, especially when the king took seven different helmets about with him as Edward II did.

Then there was the marshal and his department which made all the arrangements for journeys, for the king's protection, and for the order of travel. If the court could not reach its destination in one day and had to put up somewhere for the night the marshal had the hateful job of finding enough billets for everyone. The king himself would stay in a monastery or a private castle or manor, but the rest of the household had to be pushed in anywhere, and the marshal's men went round the houses of the district marking the doors with chalk to show that they had commandeered all the beds inside, and even then many slept in the barns and outhouses. It was the marshal who paid three pence a day to the king's four horn-blowers, and to the twenty-four archers who rode just ahead of their royal master to protect him, and he also must have paid five pence a day to the cat-hunters and three pence to the bearward who were members of the royal household.

The department of the chancellor was in some ways the most important section of the court. Under him were the king's chaplains who said daily services for him. Each of them had a boy to attend to him, and besides his daily food received money for robes, shoes, and laundry, and two red serges (blankets) for his bed. Besides the chaplains there were clerks who wrote the royal letters, charters, and proclamations, and all the other documents connected with the government of the country. They were often the only people who could write, and for this reason many men from the chancellor's department rose to important positions, while the chancellor himself was the highest official in the kingdom.

The heads of all these departments were noblemen, except the chancellor who was a churchman. Each had under him a little army of lesser servants, cooks, butler, water-bearers, keepers of hounds and hawks, huntsmen, and grooms, and even laundresses, who all had to be fed and paid, and given orders as well as taken about wherever the court went. The officials of the royal household must have been exceedingly busy men.

With the king and queen, besides these high officials, there were members of their own family and their friends. Edward III was sometimes attended by no fewer than five hundred knights, fifteen of whom were 'new made', and his mother had sixty ladies and damosels. Their personal attendants also included pages and squires. The pages were the sons of noblemen, as we already know, and were being educated for knighthood. The squires had many different duties according to the department they were in. Geoffrey Chaucer, the poet, became a squire of the bedchamber to Edward III in 1372. He had to take turns to watch the king in case he wanted anything, and to be ready at all times to take messages. In the afternoon and evening his duties were to attend in the private apartments, and talk, or sing, or play on the harp or pipe, and generally to amuse people. Especially he had to look after strangers who did not know the ways of the court. Sometimes he would take part in pastimes in the woods or by the river, or on colder days would play at chess or backgammon indoors. He also had to serve wine to the king on bended knee, and taste the food before meals for fear of poison. For all this Chaucer's wages were seven pence halfpenny a day, but besides that he had two suits of clothes a year, and one of these we know was a very fine one with red and black stockings. He also had his food, a daily ration of bread, a helping of the main dish at all meals, a gallon of beer, and a bundle of firewood and two good candles in winter. He shared a bed with another squire in a small room, which was great luxury, for many squires simply slept on the floor of the hall wherever the court happened to be staying.

The king himself was a knight and so were all the great nobles of his realm. So, too, were the great mass of the gentry, who were trained in arms, and knew something of courtly and generous behaviour. It was the ambition of every gentle-born page and squire to become a knight, and, if possible, to be admitted to one of the famous orders of chivalry. Of these probably the best known was the Order of the Garter which was founded by Edward III in 1344. Edward himself was the most famous knight of his time, 'glorious among all the great ones of the world'. He was said to be 'great-hearted, and generous in giving, prudent in counsel, gentle in speech, and pitiful to the afflicted', though when we hear of his treatment of the men of Calais in 1346, this sounds rather odd. But compared with other great men of his time he was certainly kindhearted and honourable. Of his bravery there was no doubt, in war he feared nothing, raging like a wild boar in the thick of the fight and shouting, 'Ha St. Edward' and 'Ha St. George'. In peace time he kept splendid state, and appeared at Windsor dressed in white and silver, his tunic embroidered with a swan and his motto in gold,

Hay Hay the White Swan
By Goddes soul I am thy man.

Even older than the Order of the Garter was the knightly Company of the Bath, and long and solemn was the ceremony

EDWARD III CREATES A KNIGHT

Even today the king strikes the new knight lightly across the shoulder with a
drawn sword

of admitting a new member. He had to be a squire, well trained in courtesy and arms, a skilful horseman, and of good character. The night before the ceremony of knighting the candidate was taken by two other squires into a chamber where he was shaved, had his hair cut and was put into a large bath, carefully covered over with a blanket and tapestry, 'against the coldness of the night'. One of the squires knelt before the bath-tub, and said in a soft voice, 'Sir, be this bath of great honour to you and wash away your sins.' He was then put into bed, not to go to sleep but to get dry! After this he was taken out of bed, and 'cloathed very warm' by the squires, who seem to have been terrified of his catching a chill, which is not to be wondered at as he then had to spend the night in church which was extremely cold, praying through the dark hours with a taper burning on the altar before him. Very early in the morning, after service of Mass had been said, the squires carefully dressed him, and he was led into the presence of the king by all the other Knights of the Bath. Before him went a squire bearing a sword in a white leather scabbard, with a belt of the same, a pair of golden spurs hanging on the hilt. Then the king took the sword and touched his shoulder with it, and the spurs and touched his heels, kissed him and said, 'Be thou a good knight.' After that the company went happily to dinner.

If a knight committed a very serious crime, such as treason or flying from battle, he could be degraded, and turned out of his Order in fearful shame. His spurs were hacked off his heels, his coat of arms was pulled off, torn in pieces and scattered to the four winds, and his armour was banged and beaten till it was all dented and smashed and then thrown into the nearest ditch. Finally he was given another surcoat with his arms upside down upon it. *Vale proditor* (Bah, traitor!)—was written beside his name in the register of the Order and he was driven forth never to return.

But the court of the king was not occupied only with such ceremonies as these and with revels. A great deal of hard work went on there, too. It was the place from which all England was governed. One of the busiest departments was the Treasury or as it came to be called the Exchequer, for it not only guarded the royal jewels and treasure but also dealt with the money that came in from all over the land, money which was collected and paid in twice a year. For a long time the Treasury travelled with the king but this was found very awkward and not particularly safe, and Henry II decided that it had better remain in one place. He first chose Winchester, but later it settled in Westminster. There came the sheriffs with their money bags. A sheriff was an important man who looked after the king's affairs in each county. At Easter and again at Michaelmas he paid in what he had collected in taxes half at a time. The money was very carefully tested to make sure that the king was not being cheated. First it was counted and a note of the amount made. But in those days it was a very common thing for men who wanted to steal the silver without being caught to clip or shave round the edge of coins so that they were not really worth the correct amount, a thing which we now prevent by making them, the silver ones at any rate, with milled edges. After being counted therefore the money was weighed. Now two hundred and forty silver pennies were supposed to go to one pound in weight. If it was found that the pennies were too light, that perhaps two hundred and forty-eight were required to tip the scales down at a pound, then the unhappy sheriff had to make up the difference, and produce the extra eight silver pennies from his own purse. But even counting and weighing were not considered enough. The coins were also tested to see if they were made of pure metal. A small handful taken from any of the sheriff's money bags was melted down, and, if there was too much dross and too little silver, he again had to put his hand in his pocket to make up the amount. The sheriff was given a receipt for the sum he paid in, but not a paper one as we have today, for there was no paper then and parchment was too expensive. So he was given what was called a tally. This was a piece of wood, usually hazel, and shaped like a small cricket bat. Along its edges the clerks in the exchequer cut notches to represent the amount received. These notches were of different sizes, and when people understood the plan they could read a sum off a tally as quickly as you can read £1,352. 16s. 8d. One thousand pounds was marked by a notch as wide as the palm of the hand, a hundred by the breadth of the top part of the thumb, a pound by the breadth of a grain of ripe barley, a shilling a smaller triangular notch, and a penny by a straight cut, nothing being taken out of the wood. Then the tally was split down the middle, the sheriff took one half away with him and the other was in the exchequer. If any argument arose afterwards the two halves could be put together and made to 'tally', that is, to agree. You can see from the picture what tallies were like— they were used as receipts for hundreds of years, in fact they did not disappear completely until 1826. Piles of them lay in the cellars of the House of Commons. In 1834 a workman was given orders to burn them, which he did on the stove of the House of Lords. The dry old wooden receipts made such a blaze that the fire spread through the building and destroyed almost the whole of the Houses of Parliament.

There was another very important side to the work of the king's court. From very early times it had been the place where

THE EXCHEQUER COURT

Weighing a pound of silver money before witnesses. The man on the right
of the picture holds a tally

men came for justice. There the king, sometimes alone and
sometimes with the great men of his realm about him, listened
to those who came to him with complaints, pleas, and accusa-
tions, and having heard both sides gave judgement. When the
king was himself skilful and learned in the law of the land, as
Henry II and Edward I were, his decisions were about the
fairest men could get, but this was not always the case. A weak
king or one who was not interested in trials and judgements,
was not so satisfactory as a judge. And then, too, the court as
we know was perpetually on the move, and the danger and
expense of trailing around England after a rapidly moving king
was altogether too much for many people. So gradually the
custom grew up of leaving a certain number of trained judges
behind in Westminster, who sat in the king's palace there to

hear the pleas of any lords and freemen who brought their cases to them. When the court happened to be at Westminster Palace the king would hear some of the cases, usually the most important ones between great nobles or clergy, though Henry II certainly listened to the pleas of humble freemen as well as to those of mighty barons and bishops. But even to go to London was out of the question for many people who could not afford it, or who feared to make so great a journey. Some simply could not be away from home for long, even if they were sure of getting a hearing and not being sent off after the royal court which might be in Oxford one week and in the Welsh Marches the next. Henry II in particular, who knew the great importance of law and order, realized that if the people could not come to the court, then the court—at least that part which would judge

In the fourteenth century clothes became more elaborate and were made of much richer materials. Older men and important officials wore long robes

cases well and fairly—must go to them. He issued a famous declaration in 1166, called the Assize of Clarendon, and ordered, as we have seen in Chapter 6, that certain of his judges were to travel about the country and hear cases and give justice in the king's name. This system still goes on to this day. Three times a year, in winter, summer, and autumn his Majesty's judges travel about England and Wales in eight circuits or districts, and hold *assizes*, as their courts are called, in various places. Sometimes there is a special house in which the travelling judge always stays, sometimes he stays at the mayor's house, and anyone who lives in an assize town can watch him in his robes and his great wig driving or possibly just walking to hear the cases.

15. Edward III and the Hundred Years War

EVER since 1066, when William of Normandy became William of England, too, the kings of England had owned lands in France. These were at their greatest under Henry II who had been master of all the western half of the land, as you will remember if you look back at the map on page 79, a fact which was naturally very much disliked by French kings. The connexion between the two countries was very important to England. For one thing, it made the Plantagenet kings far more powerful than if they had been only the rulers of a small and rather isolated island, and for another, it brought a great deal

HEADPIECE. Edward III. When he claimed the throne of France, he combined the lilies of France and the leopards of England into his personal shield

of French influence into this country. Many tough vigorous new inhabitants—the Normans—came over to settle here, not only barons and knights who held estates, but also merchants, like Gilbert à Becket, the father of Thomas the archbishop, came for trade. And of course these Frenchmen brought their language which, with Latin, became for hundreds of years the polite, as well as the official, tongue, so that a man who could only speak English was either of no importance at all or else was laughed at as a very uncouth person. Very slowly the French speech became absorbed into the tongue of Harold's England, but there are many words, phrases, and names still in use which remind us that we were once very closely linked with France. If you remember this, you will not be so surprised when you hear that even now the king of England gives his formal consent to an Act of Parliament with the French phrase *Le roy le veult*—the king wills it—nor when you read in Chapter 9 of the cry *Gardez l'eau*.

The English lands in France included parts of the warm dry south specially suitable for growing grapes from which splendid wine was, and still is, made, and an important trade in this grew up between the two countries. Every year merchants of the port of Bordeaux shipped hundreds of casks to London, Southampton, and Bristol; and many an Englishman who had once been content with home-brewed ale and mead learned to enjoy the wine of France whenever he could afford it. In exchange English merchants gained foreign markets for their goods. Their wool was much the best and most eagerly sought after in all Europe, and besides wool they also sold leather and sheepskins. Altogether there was much coming and going across the Channel, and the merchants, both French and English, learned to be free of each other's country and to exchange habits, and fashions in clothes and food, and new ideas as well as goods. For men, speech, and trade were not the only things that England gained from being closely connected with richer and more civilized France. The songs of minstrels and poets, the writings and thoughts of scholars, the architecture of castles and churches were all influenced by it. It was quite possible to hold important posts in both countries; for instance a certain Henry de Galeys was lord mayor of London in 1274 and mayor of Bordeaux in 1275.

After the death of Henry II the English lands in France were never so great again. John Lackland lost the fair provinces of Normandy, Brittany, Maine, Anjou, and at last only Gascony and Guienne remained. But still the very fact of the English being on French soil at all was a bitter thing for any king of France to bear, and it is not at all surprising to find that the matter caused endless trouble. Every strong French king always tried to seize from England a little more territory, a castle here and a town there, until, by the time Edward III came to the throne of England in 1327, it was quite clear that either he would have to let Gascony and Guienne slip completely out of his grasp or fight to keep them under the English crown.

There was never much doubt about what Edward would do. He had followed his father Edward II on the throne, a man quite unsuited to be a king though he would have made an excellent and skilful farmer, for he was strong and fine-looking, and loved hedging and ditching, and looking after his horses. These country tastes of his scandalized and shocked his courtiers, and his silly behaviour cost him his crown and his life, for he was deposed and murdered in 1327. But his son Edward III was a totally different kind of man, who liked all the fashionable things, and became the hero of his people. He loved the chase,

THE COG 'THOMAS' BOUND FOR SLUYS
The sail bears the arms of the Admiral of England, Edward III (see p. 213)

the tournament, the splendid display of his court, and above all else he loved the pomp and excitement of war. Now just a year after he was crowned, a new king, Philip VI, succeeded to the throne of France, a man who was determined to drive every Englishman out of his country, and matters soon became very strained between the two. Philip began to attack Gascony and Guienne, the people of those provinces became extremely anxious about their good wine trade, and Edward made up his mind that he must go to war.

There were other causes, too, for a quarrel. Philip wanted to get the land of Flanders under his control, and again he found the hateful English in a very strong position, for the towns there depended for their livelihood on weaving cloth, and for their cloth they needed all the English wool they could get. Philip foolishly persuaded the count of Flanders to stop all trade between Flanders and England. Now if this had come about, the plight of the Flemish people would have been terrible, their spinners, weavers, sailors, and merchants would soon have been out of work and hungry, and not unnaturally they decided to disobey their count and to keep trade alive at all costs. But the count and Philip VI were powerful enemies to make, and so the Flemish merchants asked Edward III for his help, and took him for their overlord. To the delight of the cloth-workers of Flanders and the farmers and wool merchants of England Edward promised to defend the trade, knowing quite well that his promise would lead to war. In order to please the Flemish still more he took the title of king of France, saying that he had through his French mother a better claim to it than Philip, because Philip, as you can see from the family plan given below, was only a cousin of Charles IV who ruled before him. Edward

Edward III's Claim to the French Crown

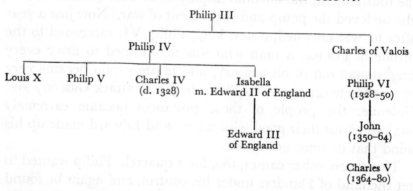

Philip III

Philip IV — Charles of Valois

Louis X · Philip V · Charles IV (d. 1328) · Isabella m. Edward II of England · Philip VI (1328–50)

Edward III of England · John (1350–64)

Charles V (1364–80)

added the lilies of France to the golden leopards of England on his coat of arms which you can still see on his tomb in

Westminster Abbey. When he wrote to Philip he addressed him as 'Philip, who calls himself the King of the French', which was obviously very insulting.

So in 1337 for these three causes—the lands in France, the trade with Flanders, and his pretended claim to the French crown—Edward III began a war, which lasted off and on for over a hundred years and caused untold misery to thousands of people. But to begin with, in England at least, the barons, the knights, and the freemen were delighted at the prospect of fighting which they greatly enjoyed. They looked forward eagerly to adventure and a pleasant change of air, they hoped for rich plunder and large ransoms for any Frenchman they were able to capture. Indeed, the enthusiasm was so great that Parliament agreed that the king should raise big sums of money for his expenses, and all townsmen were ordered to give him one-tenth of their goods and the countrymen one-fifteenth of theirs.

Then Edward collected an army. The Norman way of doing this would have been for the king to send messages round to his tenants-in-chief, saying, 'Meet me at such and such a place and do your military service by coming to fight in France'. But this method had gone out of fashion and Edward III usually arranged with barons and knights to raise troops of soldiers for which he paid, a fully armed knight earning a shilling a day and a squire six pence. Of course such an army was utterly different from a modern one. In the first place it was very small, and in the second it usually only fought in the summer, and in the winter, when the bad weather made travelling almost impossible, it settled into winter quarters or went home. It consisted of foot-soldiers and knights on horseback. The knights, though eager and brave and well trained in fighting, were very little use except on horseback, because by the fourteenth century their armour was so heavy that it was very difficult for them to walk in it. They were always trying to make it more and more protective against improved weapons like the long-bow, and they did this by constantly adding extra pieces of metal on the most exposed parts of the body, such as the knee and arm. A knight preparing for battle in the fourteenth century really did behave rather like the Tweedles, Dum and Dee, piling on thing after thing till he could hardly move.

First he put on a tunic and breeches and a pair of strong shoes, so that the armour would not rub him and make blisters and sore places. Next he put on his hauberk and chain mail; over this garment came extra protective plate armour; the first part to go on being overshoes of metal; these had to come first because a fully armed knight would be quite unable to bend down and fasten them! Then on went the shin plates and special knee and elbow caps. Next the two main pieces of body armour, the breast plate and the back plate, were buckled round him by his squire. His arms were covered in two parts, from wrist to elbow, and elbow to shoulder, and he pulled on gauntlets of steel. Finally somebody fastened him into his helmet, which he could not possibly manage for himself, and put on his surcoat; this was a sleeveless tunic of linen or silk with his coat of arms embroidered back and front, and it was very important for it was the only way of recognizing a man who was completely hidden inside his armour. Then the knight moved off to battle—as well as he could. If he had the misfortune to be unhorsed he usually lay helpless on the ground, until a friend came and dragged him to his feet again, or an enemy made him prisoner, and having settled the question of the ransom, removed his sword, and helped him up. Sometimes

ARMING THE BLACK PRINCE

Two squires are fastening his breast-plate while two more are holding his sword,
surcoat, and helmet. The other parts of his armour are lying ready. One of the
shields hanging up was 'for war', and the other 'for peace'

if nobody helped him he even suffocated inside his armour, so he was glad to get up at almost any cost. During the Hundred Years War much money was made out of such ransoms. Edward III paid £16 as part of the ransom for his squire Geoffrey Chaucer, and to buy a knight's freedom would be much more expensive.

The foot-soldiers were mostly archers armed with their long-bows, and undoubtedly they were most important men in the army. They were not covered with metal like the knights, but wore stout leather jackets and steel caps, and they earned three pence a day. On the right forefinger an archer wore a stout leather finger-stall so that the constant plucking of the bowstring should not make it sore and he had his left wrist covered with a leather guard, called a 'bracer', to protect it from the friction of the arrow as it flew out from the bow. They usually stole their food from wherever they could. Each man carried his own bow and looked after it tenderly. It was about as tall as he was, made of springy yew or elm-wood, with a tough bow-string of hemp. Both bow and string had to be kept supple and dry—it was a disgrace to let them get wet—and their owners rubbed and polished them very carefully with wax and resin. The arrows were 2 feet 6 inches long, and there was always a great deal of argument about the best way of feathering them, that is, about how the feathers which helped their flight should be fastened on and shaped. But most archers agreed about the best kind of feathers to use—the quills of the grey goose, which had fallen, not been pulled from a three-year-old bird. The English archers had a great advantage over the French because they were using the long-bow, while their enemies still had the cross-bow which took longer to work and had a much shorter range, so that often before the French cross-bowmen could get near enough to the English army to shoot effectively, they were themselves shot down. And the art of using the long-bow was so difficult that they never learned it, so that the English archers were on top all through the war.

Edward III took the usual weapons of war with him, machines for hurling stones and burning-pitch balls among the enemy, scaling-ladders, and battering-rams, but he also took a few cannon, for gunpowder had been introduced into England early in his reign. These cannon created a great impression by the noise they made, but as they were apt to explode when fired, they sometimes seem to have done quite as much damage to their owners as to the enemy. They were, in the end, to make all the protective armour of knights quite useless and to put the archers out of work, but that was not to happen for another three hundred years.

For some time before war broke out the French had been raiding the south coast of England, doing great damage as well as terrifying people. Portsmouth, Southampton, Winchelsea, Rye, Hastings, and Dover had been attacked and burnt, as well as smaller places in Devon and Cornwall. Up and down the coast fishermen bewailed their boats and nets, and farmers their corn-stacks and animals. In 1340 Edward determined to put a stop to such things by crippling the French shipping. With a rather ragged collection of two hundred ships, mostly armed merchant ships, he attacked the French as they lay in the Channel near the port of Sluys. His navy came chiefly from the five Cinque Ports of Dover, Romney, Sandwich, Hastings, and Hythe. These towns had the duty of providing the king with fifty-seven ships and thirteen hundred men for fifteen days at their own expense. If he needed them for a longer period he had to pay for them himself. There were also a certain number

of royal ships—one of which, called the *Christopher*, had been captured by the French just before the battle of Sluys—and a good
many belonging to ordinary merchants who were willing to hire
their craft to the king. All these ships were very much alike,
they used sails, not oars, they were gaily painted, and at each
end had a high poop. The three chief officers were the master,
the constable, and the steersman, and all were sailors and knew
the Channel well. For the rest the ship was filled with fighting-
men, and the usual method of warfare was to come alongside the
enemy ship, throw grappling hooks over the gunwale, and
fasten the two together, and then swarm aboard and fight hand
to hand. Edward's fleet was actually slightly bigger than that
of the French, yet when he came within sight of the enemy as
they lay off the coast of Flanders he saw so great a number of
ships that their masts seemed to be like a great wood. But the
sight did not seem to disturb the king. He merely said to the
master of his own ship, 'Ah! I have long desired to fight with
the Frenchmen, and now shall I by the grace of God and St.
George, for truly they have done me many displeasures.' Then
he drew his fleet off a little to get both wind and sun behind
him, while the French, keeping the captured *Christopher* in a
position where the English could not fail to see her, blew their
trumpets and instruments, and waited in three lines for the
onslaught. Sir John Froissart, who was secretary to Queen
Philippa of England and wrote a history of the war, says that
the battle was 'right fierce and terrible', and adds that he thinks
battles on the sea are more terrible than on land because no one
can run away. No one could get back again either, if they fell
overboard. The battle went on from early morning till it was
dark, and though the English endured much pain, for their
enemies were four to one and all good men on the sea, they

were victorious, and the French fleet was almost entirely
destroyed. Then Edward returned home in triumph and to
celebrate he struck a gold coin called a noble, bearing on it
a ship and the words *Ihesus autem transiens per medium illorum ibat.*
This was one of the earliest gold coins to be used in England,
besides it there were only silver pennies, two hundred and forty
of them to one pound in weight, and groats, which were four-
penny pieces.

After the battle of Sluys the war took the form of large-scale
raids by the English army on France, much more terrible than
the French ones on the south coast of England. Edward III
allowed his soldiers to plunder and rob everywhere they went
till the very name of Englishman was hated and feared. Sir
John Froissart, in his history of the war, paints unpleasant
pictures of their behaviour, saying that they stole or burnt everything, 'barns full of corn, houses full of riches, carts, horses,
swine, muttons, and other beasts'. And he shows us plainly one
of the reasons why the war was popular with the invading army
by saying, 'the soldiers made no count to the king . . . of the gold
and silver they did get; they kept that to themselves'. And if
you look at them at work in the picture on page 215, you can
imagine that they kept a good deal to themselves, and that many
beautiful things found their way back to England—tapestries,
jewels, cups and candlesticks, feather beds and sheets—and that
many Englishwomen began to appear in clothes which had once
been worn in France. In this way the good and fruitful land of
Normandy was wrecked by Edward's army.

It was after one of these raids in August 1346 that Edward,
moving northward towards the coast, found himself near the
small village of Crécy with the French army hard on his heels.
It was soon perfectly clear that he could not shake them off, for

his own men were hungry and tired out with the march, since the weather had been very bad and the tracks were heavy with water and mud. He therefore chose as good a position as he could and prepared to make a stand. During the day there had been a bad thunderstorm, but late in the afternoon the rain stopped and the sun came out, shining from behind the English army straight into the eyes of the oncoming enemy. The French knights, loaded with armour and splendidly mounted, were certain that they would win the battle by one or two magnificent charges against the English lines. But, unfortunately for them, they never reached those lines. Before they could do so their own ranks were broken again and again by the horrifying arrows of the English bowmen, as they stood fair and easily on their feet, and quite undaunted by the shouts and yells of the enemy archers who were using cross-bows and never got near enough to shoot. Indeed, the English shot so thick and fast that the arrows fell like a snowstorm on to the French. Their horses crashed to the ground or reared and bolted, the knights fell, lay helpless, and were trampled to death. Fifteen times on that sultry August evening did the French charge, and only once did they look like being victorious. That was when they reached the company commanded by Edward's eldest son, the Prince of Wales. The young prince himself was unhorsed but managed to rally his men and drive back the French. By nightfall the first great battle of the Hundred Years War was over and the English were the victors. The day had been won by the bowmen, but the French did not seem to realize this, for they did not try to adopt the long-bow but went on using the cross-bow and the knightly charge for the rest of the war, and very ill they fared through it.

Then Edward and his army, having lost only a few hundred men to the four thousand of the enemy, marched on in good

THE HUNDRED YEARS WAR
English soldiers sacking a French town. The ordinary people of France were the real sufferers from the Hundred Years War

spirits to the coast and settled down to besiege the town of Calais.

Now Edward hated Calais with all his heart, for it was the nest and safe haven of the pirates who raked the Channel for English ships and who raided the coast of England, and he was determined to capture the city and clear the nest once and for all. It was very strongly fortified and had the sea on one side which of course made a siege much more difficult. Edward did not mean to waste the lives of his men by violent attacks on so strong a place, and instead of setting to work to mine the walls, and bombard them with the various machines he had with him, he simply encircled it and waited. He felt sure he could starve the people into yielding. He built quarters for his army all round the town on the landward side, wooden huts thatched with reeds and broom, so numerous that it seemed that a new town had sprung up. There were shops for bread, wine, and clothes, and a market was held twice a week where the soldiers could buy what they wanted. On the seaward side many small watchful English ships guarded the entrance to the harbour so that no help might come that way. Only on foggy nights did two brave Frenchmen, named Marant and Mestriel, who knew the coast and harbour well, manage to slip through occasionally with a little food to comfort the people of Calais. But in spite of this their stocks fell lower and lower till they were eating dogs, cats, nettles, and rats. Then the governor sent out from the city gates seventeen hundred poor old people and young children for whom he had no longer any food, hoping that they might be allowed to pass through the English lines. For once Edward showed pity for the helpless, gave them food and drink and let them go freely.

The siege went on all through the winter of 1346 until the governor realized that no help could reach him and his task was hopeless. King Philip of France had once marched within sight of the city but daunted by the size of the English host he had disappeared again. Then the governor sent to Edward and offered to give the town into his hands if he would promise to let the remaining garrison go free. At first Edward bluntly refused saying he would have Calais without any conditions attached and no one should go free, but after much persuasion he changed his mind and promised that if six of the chief burgesses came forth bareheaded, barefooted, barelegged, and dressed only in their shirts, with ropes about their necks, and the keys of the town in their hands, and gave themselves up to his mercy, he would let the rest go free. Then the governor accepted these terms, and forth came the six men and kneeled before the king who looked bleakly upon them, and because of his great hatred for the town of Calais ordered that their heads should be cut off. In vain Edward's own knights begged him to have mercy on them and not to blemish his good name, but he turned his back and would not listen. At last there came his queen, Philippa, the most liberal and gentle woman of her day, and begged him to relent. Edward, who was devoted to his wife, could not refuse her and he gave the six burgesses into her hands to treat them as she liked. She let them go, first giving them each a new suit of clothes and six gold coins. Then the English took possession of Calais, and kept it, a little island of territory, for two hundred and fifty years.

Crécy and Calais were triumphs for the English, and they won another great victory at Poitiers in 1356 when the king of France himself was taken prisoner and brought to England while his ransom was being collected. But these successes were not enough to conquer the whole of France and so the raids went on year after year. Edward III soon left the command of the army to the Prince of Wales, who was a good soldier, but a hard and haughty man. Although his knights admired him and thought him a pattern of bravery and fighting skill, and although he could behave most courteously to a fallen enemy of his own class, yet in his treatment of poor people and helpless refugees he was completely merciless. He was called the Black Prince, and the name has stuck to him to this day. It may have been given to him because he wore black armour, but it is more likely that he earned it by black temper and black deeds.

After 1370 the prince became so ill that he had to be carried everywhere in a litter, for he was too weak to sit astride his horse, and in 1376 he died leaving a little son Richard as his heir. By then much of the land in France which the English army had won since Crécy had been lost again, for it was far too small to hold it all against the French, and when Edward III himself died in 1377 only Calais and Gascony remained in English hands.

THE BURGHERS OF CALAIS
bringing the keys of the town to Edward III, 1346

16. Changes and Troubles

YOUNG Richard II came to the throne in 1377 at a troubled time. For the last few years the war with France had been going badly; Edward III had been childish with age and the Black Prince a sick and exhausted man, and the lands they had conquered began to slip out of their hands again. But this was not all; at home, too, there were many difficulties, and changes were going on which needed a period of peace if they were to happen without grave trouble. These changes were bound to come. It was now more than three hundred years since the Conquest, and the life of a country and its people can never stand still. If you think just of the place you live in and the people you know, you can easily think of a whole list of alterations which have happened in quite a short time. Old houses

HEADPIECE. Escaping from the Black Death

may have been demolished and new ones built, perhaps in quite a new style, fashions in clothes have changed, the work people do and the tools they do it with, whether a tractor or a fountain-pen, may be different. You may also be able to think of places which instead of growing have become smaller since you knew them.

Now in the twentieth century such changes appear much more rapidly than they did in the Middle Ages, and you might think that outwardly a village in 1377 was exactly the same as in 1077, but you would be wrong. Certainly the houses were not very different, though possibly a few more of them had two rooms instead of one, or had added a lean-to shed at the side to house the animals, or store the corn. The manor house would look unchanged from the outside, but if you went in you would almost certainly find that the fire had been moved from its place in the middle of the hall, and now burned on a hearth against one of the walls, and that there was a stone chimney for the smoke to escape by and a stone hood projecting from the wall to draw it up. The windows might have glass in them, and there might well be tapestry or painted cloths hung on the walls. The lord still travelled from manor to manor to eat up the produce of each one, and his steward looked after the estate when he was away and held the manor court every three weeks or so. Round the village the big open fields still lay, where the villagers had their strips and grew their food. Instead of oxen horses would probably be pulling the ploughs and carts, shod with the newly invented iron shoe and wearing much-improved harness. The rigid horse-collar which we know today was invented in the Middle Ages, so horses for the first time in history were able to pull really heavy loads without almost strangling themselves. Almost every village now had a watermill or a windmill in which corn could be ground much more quickly than by the earlier hand-mills. But apart from these changes nothing looked startlingly different, and yet if you had slipped into the hall of the manor and listened to the business of the court you would probably have spotted an important change. At first it might all seem normal. 'Nicholas Skip', says the steward, 'you are to answer in this court because forty of your sheep were found at night in the lord's oats. How will you amend this trespass? You must make (pay) fine.' 'Oh Sir, it was not on purpose, yet I will amend it' says Nicholas and he is told the amount of his fine. Next the steward calls Alice Broke-dish and says, 'Alice, you have let your house wall decay, are you ready to repair it?' 'Oh Sir', answers Alice, 'Ready am I indeed to repair it.' 'Then this court gives you three weeks to do so.' But the next piece of business might make us prick up our ears. A certain Peter Pottage is taking over his father's strips in the open fields. He pays his heriot to the steward—a stiff one of two cows—and then calmly says that he will pay his lord four pence a year for every acre that he holds. Naturally one would expect the steward to refuse this at once and demand the usual well-known services of three days' week-work, and boon-work at busy times, together with dues at special seasons. But instead, after a certain amount of haggling and argument, he agrees to it, only adding emphatically the words 'At the lord's pleasure' to the agreement. Now this is clearly a very important change, for it means that Peter Pottage is paying a money rent for his land as farmers do now, and is escaping from the services which villeins had been bound to give and which often irked them so much. It was a change which had been very slowly appearing all over the south and east and midlands of England for a long time. For instance, on the royal manor of

King's Langley in Hertfordshire by Edward I's reign (1272–1307) the villeins *either* reaped for the king *or* paid him three shillings and a penny and they either hoed for him or paid him six shillings and eight pence. With the money the lord, or his steward, would hire men to work on the demesne, who came more willingly and worked much harder because they were paid wages, and were not hankering all the time to be working on their own strips. This change to paying money rent instead of service is called commutation, and it had been happening wherever villeins had money to pay. Of course there were disputes and rows in some places about it; one lord might be willing to agree and see the advantages of the arrangement, and another might hate the idea and utterly refuse to consider it, but on the whole the process went on quietly and without much fuss, though there was naturally deep discontent among those villeins whose lords were obstinate.

Then in 1348 had come the Black Death. It came at a time when England seemed in a glorious state. The triumphs of Crécy and Calais had exalted all men and had been celebrated by feasting, dancing, tournaments, and revels of every kind: many soldiers, from noble knights to humble bowmen, had made fortunes from plunder and the ransoms of their prisoners. Edward III and his son the Black Prince were famous throughout Europe for their exploits, and England basked in the bright sun of their splendour. But along the trade routes from the East there crept a dark cloud—the plague. It moved relentlessly through Italy, Spain, and France, and in August 1348 it reached England and a man died of it at Melcombe Regis in Dorset. Now plague was not new to England, but this attack was the most terrible ever known because it was so deadly—people sometimes died a few hours after

THE SAVOY PALACE WAS THE HOUSE OF JOHN OF GAUNT

It lay between the River Thames and what is now called the Strand, and was sacked by the rebels under Wat Tyler in 1381

catching it—and because it spread so rapidly. From Dorset it went west into Devon, north to Bristol and Gloucester, then to Oxford, London, and the east, and later over the border into Scotland. When, by 1350, it died down, only about half the people of England were left alive, grass grew in the streets of towns, villages were almost deserted, crops rotted in the fields because there were so few left to creep out and gather them in. There was the same amount of land to till, but now only half the men to do it, and their work became very valuable. Some lords put their estates down to grass and kept more sheep, for this needed fewer workers than ploughing, sowing, and reaping. Many others thought that the only way to manage was to go on with the old method of granting land in exchange for service so that they could be sure of getting their villeins to work for them. Everywhere lords refused to consider commutation and tried to force men back into villeinage; everywhere the people hated the old system more bitterly because they had begun to escape from it, and grumbled and slacked at their week-work and on boon-days. In towns the journeymen struck for higher wages because they knew that there, too, men were scarce, and it was difficult for the masters to get the work done. The lords and masters of such discontented men in town and village were determined to stop their demands, and laws were passed to do this. In 1349 and again in 1351 the Statute of Labourers ordered that wages should be exactly the same as before the Black Death, and that villeins were not to ask for commutation. In order to make these orders bearable they also said that prices of food, clothes, and other necessary things were to be fixed, since if prices stayed down there could be no burning need to ask for higher wages.

There were other difficulties in England besides the misery and discontent caused by the Black Death. Although many people still reverenced the Church, which played so big a part in their lives, men of all ranks had begun to feel that all was not well with it, and that reform should be made. One man in particular felt so strongly about this and spoke so earnestly that people paid a great deal of attention to his words even if they did not always agree with him. This was John Wycliffe who was born near Richmond, Yorkshire, about 1330. He went to Oxford to take his degree and stayed on there to teach, becoming well known and much admired as a good scholar and as head of Balliol College. When he was about 40 years old he began to speak out about the evils that he saw in the Church, and did so bluntly and passionately. He attacked the great wealth of the Church, the lives of laziness and luxury led by some of the clergy. He denounced priests who spent their lives working for the king or the nobles and not at their real work of teaching people about God and his Son. Monks, priests, and friars, he said, were all too greedy for money, and were unfaithful to the example of Christ. John Wycliffe's preaching attracted great attention. There were many men who felt as keenly as he did that the Church ought to be reformed to fit it better for its tremendous task. There were others, less pleasant people, who enjoyed his attacks upon its wealth and power because they were envious and hoped that if enough trouble was stirred up some of that wealth might come their way.

John Wycliffe did not only preach about the need for reform. About 1380 he began to make a careful translation of the Bible into English so that people who could not understand Latin could read it in their own tongue, and not have to rely only on what the clergy told them about it. He began to send some of his followers out to spread his ideas all over the land. These men were known as the Poor Preachers, and were nicknamed Lollards, or babblers, by their enemies, and their preaching crusade had great influence. They were much listened to by the common people, and many of them began to go further in what they said than their master. Wycliffe certainly believed that bishops and monasteries ought not to be so wealthy, and that their riches ought to be spent in better ways than on luxurious and splendid living, but many of the Lollards, especially the more excitable ones, went a great deal farther and declared that wealth should be taken from all rich men and given to the poor, and as they preached this on the village greens of England to audiences of very poor, and sometimes extremely hungry people their words were marked with passionate interest and passed on from mouth to mouth in many cottages and ale-houses. One such speaker was John Ball, the mad priest of Kent as he was called, who spoke in a way that his betters thought very dangerous indeed, and who was constantly in trouble. 'My good friends', he would say, 'things cannot go well in England until everything shall be in common, and until the lords be no more masters than we are. Are we not all descended from the same parents, Adam and Eve? How comes it that the lords are clothed in velvet and fine stuffs while we are forced to wear poor cloth—that they have handsome manor houses when we must brave the wind and rain?' These were exciting thoughts, and it is no wonder that a jingle was made from John Ball's words and went up and down the land as:

> When Adam delved and Eve span
> Who was then a gentleman?

Now as long as the Hundred Years War went well nothing serious happened as the result of the growing discontent of the poor, but by 1380, when King Richard had been on the throne for three years, it was going very badly. Gloomy news came constantly from France, telling how the conquered lands were being lost, French sailors were again attacking English ships at sea, French soldiers were again raiding the south coast, burning the towns and villages just as they had before the battle of Sluys forty years before. Yet it never occurred to the ministers of the young king to stop the war and give their country a rest and breathing space. Instead, they went on fighting in spite of defeats, always demanding more and more money in taxes to pay for it. In 1381 they decided to demand a poll-tax of one shilling per head (or poll) from every person over fifteen years of age. This was the last straw. Everywhere the poor made desperate efforts to avoid paying, they hid themselves when the collectors came, they told lies about the ages of their children,

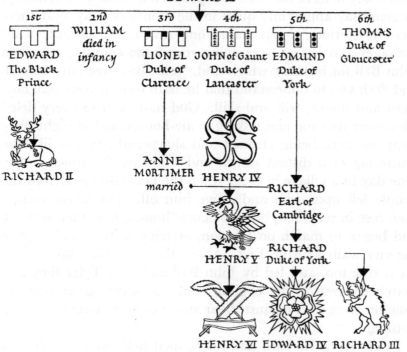

EDWARD III

1st — EDWARD The Black Prince
2nd — WILLIAM died in infancy
3rd — LIONEL Duke of Clarence
4th — JOHN of Gaunt Duke of Lancaster
5th — EDMUND Duke of York
6th — THOMAS Duke of Gloucester

RICHARD II

ANNE MORTIMER married ♦ HENRY IV

RICHARD Earl of Cambridge

HENRY V

RICHARD Duke of York

HENRY VI   EDWARD IV   RICHARD III

THE DESCENT OF THE HOUSES OF
LANCASTER AND YORK FROM EDWARD III

and when the money came to be counted it was far less than the ministers had expected and they realized that they had been cheated. Officials were ordered to tour the country and look into the matter. So they rode out with small bands of armed men ready to force the tax out of people if necessary. But though England lay apparently quiet in the month of May 1381 there were mysterious things happening under the surface. Odd messages and letters were going round the country, one from John Ball for instance which said, 'John Ball greeteth you well and doth you to understand that he hath rongen your bell, now right and might, will and skill. God haste you in every dele.' Men were meeting and talking in ale-houses, and at night rusty weapons were being cleaned and sharpened. It was like the muttering of a distant storm, and suddenly the storm broke. One day in a village in Essex when the tax collector arrived the people fell upon him and drove him off. The whole county then rose in rebellion, burned manor houses, beat their owners, and began to march on London, arriving in thousands east of the city walls at Mile End. About the same time the men of Kent rose too, and led by John Ball and Wat Tyler they also marched towards the capital. But the seven great gates of London were shut against them and they were forced to camp outside.

Inside King Richard and his council held anxious meetings in the Tower. They wanted at all costs to keep the rebels from entering the city and to persuade them to go home. But there were men in London who sympathized with them and on Thursday, 13 June, the drawbridge in the middle of London Bridge was let down and Wat Tyler and his followers surged over it. At first they roamed through the narrow streets and alleys without doing any harm, but in the afternoon their tempers rose dangerously and they poured out through Ludgate towards Westminster. Here in the fields lay the palace of John of Gaunt, uncle of the king, a man much hated by the people who believed that he was partly responsible for their troubles, especially for the poll-tax. They would certainly have killed him if he had been at home, but, as he was not, they only sacked the palace, tearing up the tapestries and grinding the golden cups and plates and jewels into the dusty road. Then they burned the whole place down. They did the same to the library and dwelling-place of the lawyers which stood a few fields away, for they hated lawyers. That night there were thousands of rebels inside the city of London, and they camped around the Tower.

Matters now looked very ugly indeed, but at this point the young king proved calmer than his councillors. Next day he rode to Mile End and interviewed the Essex men. Many actually spoke to him and begged him to grant their requests, and he agreed to do so, ordering his clerks to write a charter for the rebels. It began, 'Richard by the grace of God King of England and France [!] to all his faithful subjects—greeting.' It went on to say that the villeins were to be free of all services and were to pay their lords four pence an acre for their lands instead, also that they would not be punished for rebelling. Then most of the Essex men trudged off home believing that, as they had the promise of the king, all would be well.

But the position was still very perilous, for though the Essex rebels had gone there was still great venom abroad since Wat Tyler and his men, whose blood was inflamed by the fires they had lit and destruction they had done, were still in London. In fact, that same day they entered the Tower of London and killed the archbishop of Canterbury and the treasurer of England. Richard was obliged to sleep in a house near St. Paul's for the

Tower was thought too dangerous. Next day he arranged to meet Wat Tyler and his men and hear their grievances and demands. Early in the morning he rode past the still smoking ruins of John of Gaunt's palace to Westminster Abbey where he heard Mass and then went on to the market-square at Smithfield. The rebels were drawn up on one side of the square in hundreds, while the king's party, only about forty of them, were on the other. Then Tyler spoke to his watchful waiting followers, 'Yonder is the king', he said; 'I will go and speak with him. Stir not from hence without I make you a sign, and when I make that sign come on and slay all except the king. But do the king no harm. He is young and we will do with him as we list and so we shall be lords of all the realm without doubt.' There was only a flick of Wat's finger between the king's men and death. Then he rode over to the royal party, thrust so close to Richard that their horses were touching and began to speak to him. Now, as he spoke, a man in the king's guard cried out an insult against him, that he was a thief and a false rogue, and at this Tyler drew his dagger and made to strike the man. In a moment swords were out among the king's attendants for they were uneasy and on edge with fear and strain. Tyler was struck through the body by the mayor of London, Walworth by name, and though he turned his horse away as if to make across the square, in a moment he rolled out of the saddle, dead. Then a roar of anger rose from the rebels, bows were bent and arrows fitted, and in another instant the small royal party, an easy target standing there, would have been overwhelmed by a cloud of arrows. But in that perilous instant Richard himself spurred his horse straight forward all alone towards the furious men and cried, 'Sirs, what aileth you, and what do you seek? Do not shoot your king, for I will be your captain and your leader. Only

Showing twelfth-century fireplace   Showing fourteenth-century fireplace

MANOR HOUSE INTERIORS

follow me into yonder fields and you shall have all that you desire.' It was a piece of matchless personal courage, and of very quick thinking as well, for he led them away from the sore sight of their murdered leader, and also into the open fields where the danger of close fighting would be less. He was only fourteen at the time. There he spent the rest of the day with them granting charters, promising freedom and forgiveness, persuading them to go home, until in the evening a strong escort edged round him and rescued him, and took him back to the Tower where his mother had been waiting all day in fear for her son.

The great Peasants' Revolt was over. Next day the streets were quiet, for the leaderless peasants had departed taking with them the king's promises. But these were worthless and were never honoured. Perhaps if Richard had been his own master he might have kept his word, but he was not. Very soon on the advice, and indeed on the order, of his councillors and Parliament he withdrew the charters, and punishments, sometimes branding and torture, and sometimes death fell upon the rebels. Yet, although the peasants seemed to be beaten, in fact they were not. After the revolt it was really no longer worth the trouble and effort for a lord to hold his villeins tied to him by services and dues. He found it far better to let them hold their land for money rent and to be free men. Slow and painful had been the struggle for this freedom but it came in England sooner than anywhere else in the world.

Richard II was not blamed for the broken promises and the punishments. People felt that he was still only a boy and that his councillors were at fault. For many years, indeed, they spoke very hopefully about what he would do when he was older. But their hopes died as he grew up. He had always been odd and unusual. When he first came to the throne at the age of ten he was a sad-looking little boy with grey eyes and long brown hair. He had a strange, wild temper, and would throw his hats and shoes out of the window when he was in one of his passions. As a man he could never take things easily and became more and more self-willed and difficult to understand. He hated to be dictated to and unfortunately for him there were plenty of people who wanted to do this, Parliament for instance, and a large number of extremely powerful nobles, among them his own uncles and cousins. Richard found their advice and interference unbearable and he did everything he could to escape from it. He consulted Parliament as little as possible, he seized and imprisoned the nobles he disliked, and gradually took over control of his kingdom. Then in 1396 he made peace with France, which was the best thing he did during the whole of his reign, for it put an end to the waste of men and money which had been going on for so long and with so little good result.

But he was still afraid of his over-mighty nobles. Suddenly he began to attack them more violently. He struck down his uncle, Thomas of Gloucester, and the earl of Arundel, he exiled the earl of Warwick, the duke of Norfolk, and his own cousin Henry Bolingbroke, Duke of Hereford. At last the only important noble left was John of Gaunt, and he was old and ill. In 1399 Gaunt died, and people expected the king to recall his heir, the exiled Henry of Hereford, and allow him to live once more in England. Instead Richard seized all the vast lands and property of John of Gaunt for himself. By this time men not only feared Richard but thought he was mad. They felt unsafe with a king who could do exactly as he liked, who robbed heirs of their rightful lands, who imprisoned, exiled, or killed all those who opposed him. Away in France the banished Henry of Hereford began to think that if he came to England there would be people willing to help him regain his property from

WYCLIFFE PREACHING

his cousin Richard, and more than that, even perhaps to take that cousin's crown. He came and at once his father's tenants and many nobles flocked to join him. Richard, who was away in Ireland, hurriedly returned to save his kingdom. But his courage, once so high in Smithfield market-square, now seemed to desert him utterly. He wavered and dallied and at last, without attempting to fight, surrendered to his cousin, and gave up not only the stolen estates but the crown of England itself. Henry of Hereford was proclaimed King Henry IV, and Richard was parted from all his friends and held a prisoner in Pomfret Castle. The next year, 1400, he was murdered, and all the promise of his boyhood, and the hopes of his subjects had come to nothing.

17. Henry V and the French War

HENRY IV became king because he had the support of all the people whom Richard II had offended or injured, and because Parliament agreed to his coronation. But he was a usurper, that is he had seized the throne when it was occupied by someone else. It is true that the unpopular Richard had abdicated and that he had no children to follow him, but even so, as you can see from the family plan on page 227, the descendants of Lionel of Clarence, the third son of Edward III, should have come before Henry, descendant of the fourth. So it is not surprising that he had great difficulties to cope with, including three dangerous rebellions of barons, who hoped to drive him from the throne, and a rising in Wales, where Owen Glendower stirred up the old desire of the Welsh to be free of England, and

HEADPIECE. Henry V. The royal arms are shown at the top.

Shakespeare in the play *Henry V*, calls his reign a 'scambling and unquiet time'. Yet he managed to survive and to pass on the crown in 1413 to his eldest son. This son, Henry V, became one of the most famous kings of England but, like Richard Cœur de Lion, he was famous for things which brought little of lasting value to his subjects. When his father died he was a tall thin young man of twenty-six, with red cheeks and brown hair, which he kept cut very short over his ears as the fashion was then. In his portrait he looks rather severe and hard, and indeed he often was, for he persecuted the Lollards most cruelly and would calmly watch the poor wretches burning to death, and he did not hesitate to murder prisoners of war in cold blood when he thought it would help him. Yet Harry of England, as his subjects liked to call him, could be merry enough as he sat drinking with his friends, or when he was playing games, which all his life he loved, for he was a fast runner and could jump like a stag. Ambassadors from foreign countries were much struck by his kingly bearing and dignity, and seemed to know at once that he was not a man to be trifled with. Perhaps the best thing about him, next to his courage, was that though he could be ruthless and cruel at times he had a great interest in his subjects, even the humble ones, and liked to know what they were thinking and hoping for. Unfortunately he never used that interest or his gifts as a leader in peaceful ways, but wore himself out in useless fighting and died when he was only thirty-five.

From the first Henry's great desire was to attack France again and to end the peace which Richard II had made in 1396. He was a born soldier and longed to win back all the lands which the English had ever held in France, and if possible to conquer the whole country. He also knew perfectly well that unless his powerful nobles at home were given plenty to occupy

AGINCOURT
The destruction of the French cavalry by English arrows

them they would have time to think again about his father's seizure of the throne and to plot and rebel against himself. Their favourite occupation was war and Henry determined to give them plenty of it.

A small country like England had no real chance of conquering a much bigger one like France, especially if the French people were united under a strong king, but at this time they were not, and, in fact, their land was in a most unhappy state. The king, Charles VI, was a lunatic. One day while out riding he had suddenly drawn his sword and madly attacked the courtiers who were with him, so that for some minutes no one dared approach him. He never properly recovered his reason, and went about biting his nails and pulling out his hair. He refused to wash and it sometimes took ten men to change his clothes. This illness of Charles was a great misfortune for France, but it was not the end of her troubles. Among the great French nobles, many of whom were just as strong and powerful as the over-mighty men who had caused such trouble to Richard II and Henry IV, the greatest were the duke of Burgundy and the duke of Orleans, and between these two there was a terrible feud. Both of them owned vast estates and had many vassals and tenants who followed the example of their lords and quarrelled and fought and hated each other bitterly. France was torn in two by this feud, and when one duke was on the king's side you could be practically certain of finding the other with his enemies. They and their private armies never fought on the same side.

This state of things made France so weak that in the summer of 1415 Henry collected an army and invaded Normandy. He landed near the mouth of the River Seine and began a siege of Harfleur. The town, battered by Henry's guns, which had nicknames like the 'London', the 'Messenger', and the 'King's Daughter', gave in after five weeks. But it was not much of a triumph for him, for he had lost hundreds of men through illness, and he therefore decided to march to Calais, which still belonged to England, and sail for home to collect fresh troops. This march was very different from those of the Black Prince when burning and thieving had been the order of the day. Now the French people were amazed at the change in the English, for Henry was very particular about the behaviour of his troops and would not allow them to plunder the countryside.

As they made for Calais on a wet October evening the tired English, who had trudged all day through the muddy fields and lanes, found themselves cut off by a French army four times as large as theirs, very much as Edward III had found at Crécy in

ENGLAND AND FRANCE AT THE TREATY OF TROYES, 1420

The English king controlled the whole of the north of France as well as Gascony in
the south. With his ally, the Duke of Burgundy, he held France in a vice

1346. They camped for the night near the village of Agincourt knowing that next day—St. Crispin's Day—they must fight for their lives. The French were all followers of the duke of Orleans, for my lord of Burgundy had kept his men at home. They were mostly knights on horseback, handicapped as usual by being too heavily armed, and as usual, when the battle began, they attempted to overcome the English with their mighty charges. Just as at Crécy they were thrown into dreadful confusion by the deadly fire of the English bowmen, this time standing safely behind sharpened stakes which Henry had made them prepare. As the mass of mailed men struggled in a sea of mud, the lightly clad and nimble English fell upon them to kill or capture. The result was a victory as complete and famous as Crécy or Poitiers. In the play *Henry V*, by Shakespeare, you can read all about it, and in Oxford you can visit the college of All Souls which was built as a war memorial of Agincourt.

After the battle of Agincourt Henry went on conquering the north of France, while poor King Charles raved, his nobles quarrelled, and the common people suffered and despaired. In 1420 he had been so successful that the French were obliged to make the Treaty of Troyes. In the name of Charles, his wife promised that when her husband died Henry should become the king of France in his place and that meanwhile he should keep all the land he had won and marry her daughter the princess Catherine. Her own son, the Dauphin, was to be set aside. Then the fighting ceased and Henry returned in triumph to England, but he was already worn out with fighting and the next year, in 1422, he died, leaving a baby son of nine months old to follow him as king of England. Two months later the unhappy Charles VI died too, and the small Henry VI was proclaimed king of France as well.

JOAN FINDS THE DAUPHIN HIDING AMONG HIS COURTIERS
AT CHINON

But it was not likely that the French would accept him without a struggle, especially as their own king had left a grown-up son, the Dauphin, and so the war broke out again to decide which of the two should rule France. For the first six years things went well for the English; they were full of confidence, having beaten the French so often, and Henry V's brother, the duke of Bedford, was a good general. Also the duke of Burgundy was now openly helping him and the rest of the French had no leader. Their only hope lay in the Dauphin, but unfortunately he was useless as a leader or a soldier. He was a feeble creature of nineteen, who as a baby had been so delicate that he had three screens round his cradle to keep away draughts, and all the nursery windows padded with felt. He was also so thin that the sight of his spindly legs gave people a distinct shock, and the only thing he wanted in life was to be left alone in his palace at Chinon, and not forced to fight for the throne or to exert himself in any way. But he was not to be left in peace. In 1428 there appeared at Chinon a most unusual girl—Joan of Arc. She was then just seventeen and from her childhood she had had strange dreams and visions in which voices spoke to her, always telling her the same thing, that she was one day to be the saviour of France. It was the will of God, she believed, that she should seek out the Dauphin, lead his army to victory against the English, and crown him at the great cathedral of Rheims where all French kings were crowned. Joan was born at Domrémy in Lorraine and she was a farmer's daughter, simple and strong and tough, but she was filled with wonderful power, and she did in fact inspire the French with her own passionate faith and courage so that, led by her, they began to fight the English with new strength and determination. In 1429 under Joan's white banner the French won their first victory at Orleans, driving the English back from the town which they had been besieging for six months, and in less than a year the Dauphin was crowned at Rheims and the enemy, if not defeated, was everywhere in retreat. It was now the turn of the English to be depressed and uneasy and it was Joan of Arc, the girl in a man's armour, who put fresh heart into the French, that they feared.

To her army she was the saviour of France, but the English thought that she was a witch, for they did not believe that anyone could have changed the French soldiers so completely except through magic and sorcery. Then one day in 1430 the two armies met at Compiègne, Joan leading her troops. She was on horseback, a most conspicuous figure in her bright armour, and her enemies easily recognized her, so that when, in the press of the fight, she was cut off from her followers and surrounded, they pulled her from her horse and took her prisoner. Now the men who captured her were Burgundians, but so little did they care for France that they sold Joan to the English commander, the duke of Bedford, for ten thousand gold francs. She was put in prison and tried, not by English judges, but by a court of French clergy who, after a weary trial lasting for three months, declared that she was a heretic and a witch, and that her visions came not from God, but from the devil. On 29 May 1431 she was burnt to death in the market-place at Rouen. The Burgundians caught her, French clergy condemned her, and the English burnt her, and they all share the blame for her death. But perhaps the person who comes worst out of the whole business is the Dauphin, Charles, whom she had helped to win his crown and his kingdom, and who never lifted one of his skinny fingers to save the bravest woman in the world. Nowadays both English and French honour her for the great things she did, and when in 1940 Frenchmen were again in the most dire peril fighting for the freedom of their country, many of

THE SHIELD AND MOTTO OF JOAN OF ARC

them took as their sign the double cross of Lorraine to remind them of how Joan of Arc once fought for France and saved her nearly five hundred years before.

For although at the time her death seemed a triumph for the English, yet from that year on they fought a losing fight, and although the Hundred Years War dragged on for another twenty-two years, France had through Joan recovered her spirit and endurance; it was England who fell sick. At last, in 1453, peace was made and by that time of all the lands once owned by the English in France only Calais remained in their hands.

18. Epilogue

FOR twenty-two years after Joan of Arc was burned at Rouen the English fought on in France. But their fortunes went steadily from bad to worse while the French as steadily gained vigour and victories. The treacherous duke of Burgundy deserted the English and went over with all his followers to fight against them, and they also lost by death their best leader, the duke of Bedford, brother of Henry V. At last, as we have seen, in 1453, the long wasteful war ended, and peace was made. But it was a humiliating peace for England since only Calais remained to her.

Nor did defeat in France end all her troubles. In many ways the thirty-two years which followed (1453–85) were bleak and dreary too. Henry VI, who at nine months old had been so magnificently crowned king of England and France, had lost the throne of France and he now proceeded to lose that of England too. He was a mild, peaceful, and harmless man, 'simple and upright' his secretary, Roger of Hoveden wrote,

HEADPIECE. The buildings in the background are the two famous places of education founded by Henry VI. King's College, Cambridge, on his right, and Eton College on his left 'altogether fearing the Lord God and departing from evil'. He was married to a most unsuitable wife, Margaret of Anjou, a hard, energetic young woman interested in fighting and distinctly cruel—Shakespeare in the play *Henry VI* calls her 'the she-wolf of France'. Henry himself detested fighting, and was interested in religion and education, and he caused two great and famous places of learning to be built, Eton College at Windsor and King's College at Cambridge. This gentle, peaceable man could not control the over-mighty nobles of his kingdom, who had learned the art of war so well that they could not live in peace. When they behaved like lawless ruffians, murdered and robbed their neighbours, and rebelled against the king, he had neither the will nor strength to punish them and restore order and peace. To add to his sorrows he had inherited through his mother the strain of madness which afflicted the royal family of France.

Henry had his first attack of madness in 1453 and for a time was clearly incapable of governing the country, and soon afterwards civil war broke out. On one side were the supporters of the king, who wanted to keep control of him and use the royal powers to their own advantage. They were called the Lancastrians because they fought for the family of Lancaster. The other side were called the Yorkists and they said that Henry was not fit to rule and ought to give up the throne to their leader the duke of York, who descended from the fifth son of Edward III (Henry was descended from John of Gaunt, the fourth son).

The war lasted on and off for thirty years, sometimes one side triumphant sometimes the other. At last the family of Lancaster was defeated, Henry murdered, and his heir killed in battle, and the duke of York became Edward IV. Yet, though he reigned for twenty-two years, he did not give England security or the habit of peace, and when he died in 1483, leaving a son of twelve to follow him, violence broke out again. His brother Richard, duke of Gloucester, clever and brave but quite without pity or kindness, seized the two young princes, Edward and Richard, shut them up in the Tower of London, and had himself crowned as Richard III. If he had stopped there it is quite possible that he might have succeeded in remaining on the throne, for no one was particularly keen on the prospect of another child-king—the troubles of Henry VI's reign had been a warning to everyone—but Richard III soon overreached himself and murdered the two boys, who by right stood between him and the crown. Violence breeds violence and less than two years later, in 1485, Richard himself was fighting for his crown and his life. Another figure had appeared upon the scene to try his fortune at seizing the throne—a young man named Henry Tudor, who, after spending many years in France, arrived in Wales where he and his family had large estates. He claimed to represent the House of Lancaster, and though his claim was not a particularly strong one many Englishmen turned to him in relief, hoping for a change from the confusion and bloodshed of the last thirty years. The Welsh joined him in strength as he marched eastwards across the country to meet Richard in battle and many Englishmen did the same. On 21 August 1485 their forces met at Market Bosworth near Leicester, and it was soon clear that Henry would be the victor, for Richard's men had no spirit for the fight and many deserted him during the battle. Richard himself was killed and as he fell the fine golden circlet which he was wearing on his helmet rolled away into a hawthorne bush. Here it was found and carried to Henry Tudor, who was hailed king of England on the spot. Although people knew very little of him at the time, he was a man well able to restore peace and order, and prosperity. The long line of Plantagenet kings was finished and the House of Tudor began to reign.

The long confusing war between the rival families of Lancaster and York had lasted, as we have said, for thirty years. The armies of the two sides were never very large and fighting never went on all over England at the same time, so that a great many people did not actually fight at all or even see a battle. The most enthusiastic fighters were the barons and their followers and they suffered severely, losing much money and many lives. But this was no bad thing for England, for many of them had been far too powerful—stronger than the king himself and unwilling to obey any law except their own desires. Few dared challenge them and their neighbours often lived in fear and trembling in case they became unpopular with the local great man and suffered at his hands or those of his detestable followers. We can get a clear idea of how unsafe it was then to live in certain parts of England if we read some of the Paston letters. The Paston family lived in Norfolk, and though not noble they were wealthy and had much land and several fine houses. A near neighbour of theirs, the Lord Molynes, desired one of these houses but could not get it peacefully. So when Sir John Paston was away in London and his wife was left with only a dozen people about the place, he sent a small private army of one thousand men armed with 'curresses, briganders, jakks, salettes, gleyfes, bowes, arrows, picks, battering rams and pannys with fire' to seize it. Margaret Paston and her little band were driven out and the whole place sacked. This sort of lawlessness, for Lord Molynes was never punished, made life dangerous and uncertain for many people in all parts of the land, and it went on even in those places untouched by the civil war. A powerful government which could make all men, great, noble, and humble citizen alike, obey the laws and live at peace was urgently needed. Yet in spite of all the danger and discomfort in which a considerable number of people lived during the Wars of the Roses, towns were growing and many Englishmen were enlarging or re-building their houses and making them more comfortable. Prosperous merchants, guilds-men, and farmers, as well as noblemen, now felt that glass in their windows, and brick chimneys for their fireplaces were not unheard-of luxuries but sheer necessities, and if we can judge by the things men mentioned in their wills as being left to relations, or to churches, it is clear that at the end of the fifteenth century houses contained more furniture and were far more snug than at the beginning. They left besides fur-lined robes and silver cups, feather beds and pillows, fine coverlets, and carved wooden chairs. And here and there books are mentioned, for more people now possessed them; books, not only written by hand on parchment, but printed on paper such as in 1476 William Caxton began to produce from his printing press in London. All this was possible because, in spite of wars abroad and at home, trade had greatly increased—especially the cloth trade. Not only were the farmers in the three chief wool-growing areas—the West Riding of Yorkshire, the Cots-wolds, and East Anglia—as busy as ever rearing and shearing their sheep, but in many towns the wool was being woven into cloth in much larger quantities. Part of it still went to clothe the English people, but an increasing amount went abroad so that not only raw wool but finished cloth was exported. Many merchants like Master Greville of Chipping Campden and Master Paycocke of Coggeshall in Essex made fortunes out of the trade, and built fine new houses for themselves.

The export of cloth to the ports where foreign merchants waited for it meant that English ships went farther afield and began to take a larger part in international trade than they had ever done before, although English merchants and seamen were considered small fry compared with the Italians and Germans who carried the bulk of the eastern silks and spices and fruit from the Mediterranean, or the fur and fish and timber from the Baltic. But in the fifteenth century English traders were becoming more adventurous. They set themselves to wrest from foreigners the work of carrying merchandize to and from the ports of the Continent. And this increased activity of English merchants and seamen was highly important, for in 1492 an Italian sea-captain, Cristoforo Columbus, sailed in a ship, provided by Queen Isabella of Spain, across the Sea of Darkness, as the Atlantic Ocean was often called. He reached the West Indies and in doing so showed the way for new and adventurous voyages and trade routes. Then England's position was much more favourable. Instead of being on the outskirts of the old European routes she stood on the threshold of the new, looking out over the vast Atlantic to the Americas, and before long her merchants and seamen seized the opportunities that such a vantage point offered them.

HENRY THE SEVENTH

REFERENCE SECTION

1. THE KINGS OF ENGLAND
2. DATE CHART
3. INDEX

THE KINGS OF ENGLAND

1066–1509

1066–87		William I	The Conqueror.
1087–1100		William II	Rufus.
1100–35		Henry I	Beauclerk.
1135–54		Stephen	
1154–89		Henry II	
1189–99		Richard I	Lionheart.
1199–1216	PLANTAGENET	John	Lackland and Softsword.
1216–72		Henry III	
1272–1307		Edward I	
1307–27		Edward II	
1327–77		Edward III	
1377–99		Richard II	
1399–1413	LAN-CASTER	Henry IV	
1413–22		Henry V	
1422–61		Henry VI	
1461–83	YORK	Edward IV	
1483		Edward V	
1483–5		Richard III	
1485–1509	TUDOR	Henry VII	

		Kings of England
410	Romans leave Britain and Anglo-Saxon invasions begin	
543	St. Benedict *d.*	1016 Canute the Dane
597	St. Augustine landed	1042 Edward the Confessor
		1066 William I
632	Mohammed *d.*	
663	Synod of Whitby	
	Danish Invasions	
		1087 William II
800	Charlemagne, Emperor	1100 Henry I
		1135 Stephen
871	Alfred, king of Wessex	1154 Henry II
978	Ethelred the Redeless	
1000		1189 Richard I
		1199 John
1100		

PERIOD

1200	COVERED BY	
	THIS BOOK	1216 Henry III
1300		1272 Edward I
1400		
		1307 Edward II
1500		1327 Edward III

1509	Henry VIII, King	
1529–39	Dissolution of Monasteries	
1558	Elizabeth, Queen	
1577–80	Drake round the world	
1616	Shakespeare *d.*	
1620	Pilgrim Fathers	1377 Richard II
1642–9	Civil War	
1660	Restoration of Charles II	1399 Henry IV
1688	The Revolution	1413 Henry V
1707	Union of England and Scotland	
1714	George I, King	
1775–83	American War of Independence	
1789	French Revolution	1422 Henry VI
1793–1815	Revolutionary and Napoleonic Wars	
1837	Victoria, Queen	
1851	Great Exhibition	
1885	First motor-car	1461 Edward IV
1914–18	World War I	
	League of Nations	1483 Murder of Edward V
1939–45	World War II	Richard III
	U.N.O.	1485 Henry VII

Events in English History	Architectural Periods	Other Contemporary Events
1066 Battle of Hastings 1067 Rising at Exeter 1069 Harrying of the North 1070 Rebellion at Ely 1085 Domesday Survey	Norman	1095 First Crusade 1147 Second Crusade
1162 Becket, archbishop of Canterbury 1170 Murder of Becket 1181 Assize of Arms 1191 Richard I in Palestine		1189 Saladin takes Jerusalem 1189 Third Crusade 1193 Captivity of Richard I
1204 Loss of Normandy 1208 Interdict 1209 John excommunicated 1213 John surrenders to the Pope 1215 Magna Carta 1265 Simon de Montfort's Parliament	Early English	1226 Death of St. Francis 1265 Birth of Dante
1282 Conquest of Gwynedd (N. Wales) 1295 Model Parliament 1297 Battle of Stirling 1298 Battle of Falkirk 1314 Battle of Bannockburn 1337 Hundred Years war begins 1340 Battle of Sluys Birth of Chaucer 1346 Battle of Crécy 1348–9 Black Death 1356 Battle of Poitiers 1381 Peasants' Revolt 1384 Death of Wycliffe	Decorated	1286 Death of Alexander III (Scotland) 1292 John Balliol, king of Scotland 1306 Robert Bruce, king of Scotland
1415 Battle of Agincourt 1420 Treaty of Troyes 1431 Death of Joan of Arc 1453 End of Hundred Years War 1455 Wars of the Roses begin 1476 Caxton printing in London 1485 Battle of Bosworth	Perpendicular	1445 Invention of printing 1452 Birth of Leonardo da Vinci 1453 Fall of Constantinople 1475 Birth of Michelangelo 1492 Columbus crosses the Atlantic

INDEX

References in *italic* are to illustrations

254